Report on the Programming Language PLZ/SYS

Tod Snook
Charlie Bass
Janet Roberts
Armen Nahapetian
Mike Fay

Springer-Verlag
New York Heidelberg Berlin

Tod Snook   Janet Roberts
Charlie Bass   Armen Nahapetian
                 Mike Fay

All authors located at:

Microcomputer Systems Division
Zilog
10460 Bubb Road
Cupertino, California 95014

9 8 7 6 5 4 3 2 1

ISBN-13: 978-0-387-90374-3   e-ISBN-13: 978-1-4612-6328-9
DOI: 10.1007/978-1-4612-6328-9

PREFACE

This report describes a programming language called PLZ/SYS, which is intended to aid the implementation of system programs for microcomputers. PLZ/SYS is a synthesis of concepts from contemporary programming languages and compilers--the language Pascal has had the most notable influence on the overall design and implementation of PLZ/SYS. In order to reflect this relationship as clearly as possible, this report has been written as a heavily edited version of the revised Pascal Report. In addition to Pascal, several other languages including Euclid, Mesa, C and SIMPL, have features which have contributed to the inclusion of similar constructs in PLZ/SYS.

We wish to acknowledge both Professor N. Wirth and Springer-Verlag for their permission to use portions of the following book:

> Jensen, K./Wirth, N.: PASCAL - User Manual and Report, 2nd edition, copyright 1975 Springer-Verlag, Berlin-Heidelberg-New York

TABLE OF CONTENTS

1. INTRODUCTION

The PLZ family of languages is designed to satisfy the
requirements of a wide range of microcomputer software
development areas. This family of syntactically similar
and object code compatible language translators serves to
separate the machine-dependent aspects of a program from
the portions which are machine-independent. Thus,
selective portions of a program which are time-critical or
need explicit access to low-level machine processes may be
written conveniently without reducing the entire
programming task to this level. Furthermore, each member
of the family shares a kernel grammar defining the data
declarations and control structures for the entire PLZ
family. These common features facilitate the programmer's
transition from one language to another within the PLZ
framework. The syntactic and semantic structure of the
kernel grammar has been carefully designed to enable
efficient code generation and a simple translation process
for all the members of the PLZ family of languages.

A PLZ program is a set of modules; a module is the basic
unit of translation. A module consists of data
declarations and units of execution called procedures.
It is intended that modules be used to implement the various
data or control abstractions that comprise a program, in the
sense that modularization enables the programmer to partition
a software system into various tasks and to collect into a
single module both the data and the procedures to manipulate
that task's data. This serves to localize the scope of
attention of the programmer and reinforces "information
hiding". Inter-module communication is allowed; each module
must explicitly declare which of its procedures and/or data
are to be available for use in other modules, as well as
which procedures and/or data that are defined in other
modules are to be used in this module. Furthermore, a module
(procedures and/or data) can serve as a unit of overlay for
programs that need not be wholly present in main memory
during execution. Isolating high-frequency references within
a module reduces the potential for transfers between secondary
and primary memory.

PLZ/ASM and PLZ/SYS are examples of a low-level and a
high-level system language, respectively, from the PLZ
family. A task can be partitioned into PLZ/ASM and PLZ/SYS
modules depending on its low-level versus high-level
requirements. Once individual modules (written in
different languages within the PLZ family) have been
translated into relocatable machine code, they can be
linked together into a single program. The static and
dynamic linkage conventions between modules are facilitated
by the syntactic similarity of data declarations throughout
the family.

1.1 PLZ/SYS OBJECTIVES

The programming language PLZ/SYS has been designed to
facilitate the construction of microcomputer system
programs. A system program is one that is part of the
basic software of the machine on which it runs; such a
program might be an operating system kernel, the core of a
data base management system, or a compiler.

An important consequence of this goal is that PLZ/SYS is not
intended to be a general-purpose programming language.
Furthermore, its design does not specifically address the
problems of constructing very large programs; we believe
most of the programs written in PLZ/SYS will be modest in
size. However, the language has been designed to allow the
advantages of separate compilation, including modularization
and reduced recompilation of programs.

A system programming language designed especially for
microcomputers should have the following characteristics:

1) REINFORCE GOOD PROGRAMMING PRACTICES. Both in form
(syntax) and in meaning (semantics), a high-level language
can facilitate the programming process by being readable
and clearly defined and by providing a natural
representation of algorithms. A language whose syntax is
complicated by excessive, illogical, or irregular notation
is difficult to learn and leads to repeated compilation
errors. A language whose semantics are unclear can lead to
obscure logical errors. A language whose primitive
operations are not suitable for representing the solution
to a problem can introduce errors in mapping from the known
solution to a computer program.

2) MANAGE COMPUTING RESOURCES. The details of resource
management (register and memory allocation in particular),
both during the creation and the execution of a program are
a critical aspect of the programming process. By managing
these details, a programming language can free the
programmer to think more about the problem to be solved and
less about the state of the machine. On the other hand, if
the management of resources is either inappropriate or
inefficient for data structures, the language can interfere
with the programming process. Ideally, the programmer
should be able to control resource management to the degree
justified by the circumstances.

3) ALLOW ACCESS TO THE ARCHITECTURE OF THE MACHINE. Most
microprocessor applications require precise control of the
machine and sometimes require its full operational
capability. Forcing these precision requirements through
the filter imposed by high-level language constructs can
be awkward and prohibitive. All of the primitive elements
and operations of the machine which are available through
assembly language must be accessible. Otherwise, the
barrier created by the language can prevent a viable
solution from being achieved.

4) PRODUCE EFFICIENT CODE. Even though the costs associated
with computer memory continue to drop dramatically, memory
costs remain one of the critical items in determining the
economic feasibility of a microprocessor application due to
the multiplier effect applied to these costs when the
system is replicated. By knowing the efficiency of a
particular language translator, and by quantifying the
expense of the required memory versus the overall program
development costs, it is possible to determine the
cross-over point at which it is advantageous to use a high-
level language instead of an assembly language. In
general, the fewer times a system is to be replicated, the
more likely that a high-level language is appropriate. By
improving translation efficiency, this cross-over point
occurs at a higher replication factor, thus extending the
viability of high-level language programming to more and
more applications. In addition to satisfying space efficiency
requirements, many microprocessor programs must perform their
tasks under severe time constraints. The language should
enable the generation of execution-time efficient code without
employing extensive optimization algorithms. Constructs in
the language should reflect the relative efficiency in order
to provide the programmer with some estimate of the cost of a
particular construct or algorithm.

5) BE RELATIVELY EASY TO COMPILE. Certain characteristics
of the translation process are critically important in the
microprocessor environment. First of all, the compiler
should run on the target microprocessor. Otherwise, the
user is confronted by the expense and complexity of first
running the compiler on a host computer and then
transferring the results to the target machine. Second,
the speed of the translation process directly and
indirectly affects program development. Directly, the time
it takes to correct problems in a program is influenced by
compilation time. Indirectly, if the translation time is
excessive, the programmer is inhibited from using the
compiler to its maximum benefit and may resort to debugging
strategies which offset the advantages of using a
high-level language.

There are a number of other considerations which influenced the design of PLZ/SYS:

>It is based on current knowledge of programming languages and compilers; concepts which are not fairly well understood, and features whose implementation is unclear, have been omitted.

>Although program portability is not a major goal of the language design, it is necessary to have compilers which generate code for a number of different machines, including hypothetical (interpreter-based) computers.

>The ability to enforce strict compile-time type checking must be supported by the data declaration and type definition constructs.

>The required run time support must be minimal.

The remainder of this report contains a description of PLZ/SYS, which, for the sake of brevity, is often referred to throughout the report as simply PLZ.

2. SUMMARY OF THE LANGUAGE

This section contains a summary of PLZ. The information here is intended to be consistent with the remainder of the report, but in case of conflict the body of the report (sections 3-12) governs. Because it is a summary, many details are omitted, and some general statements are made without the qualifications which may be found in the body of the report.

2.1 DATA AND STATEMENTS

An algorithm or computer program consists of two essential parts: a description of actions which are to be performed, and a description of the data which are manipulated by these actions. Actions are described by statements, and data are described by declarations and definitions. In general, a definition specifies an identifier as a synonym for a fixed value or type, and a declaration introduces an identifier to denote a variable and associates a type with it. A data type implicitly defines a set of values and the actions which may be performed on elements of that set. The data type may either be directly described in the variable declaration, or it may be referenced by a type identifier, in which case this identifier must have been previously introduced by an explicit type definition.

All data items may take on values. A value occurring in a statement may be represented by a literal constant, an identifier which has been defined to be the same as a literal constant, an identifier which has been declared as a variable, or an expression containing values. Every variable identifier occurring in the program must be introduced by a declaration which associates a data type and, optionally, an initial value with the identifier. Every constant identifier occurring in the program must be introduced by a constant definition, which simply associates a value with the identifier. The value must be determinable at compile-time; thus the expression defining a constant must contain only literal constants, constant identifiers, and built-in operations. The association is valid only within the scope of the definition and cannot be changed therein.

Throughout this report, the word "variable" means a container which can hold different values of a specific type. A "constant" is simply a fixed value, such as the number 123. The fundamental difference is that assignment to a variable is possible.

The basic data types in PLZ are the simple types. A simple
type is either a standard simple type, or a user-defined
simple type. The standard simple data types are BYTE, WORD,
SHORT_INTEGER, INTEGER, and pointer (declared using
the symbol '↑').   Types WORD and BYTE correspond to
unsigned data values of 16 bits and 8 bits, respectively.
Types INTEGER and SHORT_INTEGER correspond to signed values
of 16 and 8 bits (two's complement representation),
respectively.   Type "pointer" is for address values which
are machine-dependent quantities.   There is a way of
writing literal constants for all five types: numbers
such as 100 or character constants such as 'A' for INTEGER,
SHORT_INTEGER, WORD, or BYTE, and NIL for pointer.

Structured types are defined by describing the types of
their components and indicating a structuring method. The
various structuring methods differ in the mechanism used
to select the components of a variable of the structured
type.   In PLZ, there are two basic structuring methods
available: array and record.

In an array structure, all components are of the same type.
A component is selected by one or more array selectors
(called array indices).   The index is computed as the value
of an expression, which may be of base type WORD, INTEGER,
BYTE or SHORT_INTEGER.   Given a value of the index type, an
array yields a variable of the component type.

In a record structure, the components (called fields) are
not necessarily of the same type.   In order for the type of
a selected component to be evident from the program text
(without executing the program), a record selector is not a
computable value, but instead is an identifier uniquely
denoting the component to be selected. These field
identifiers are declared in the record type definition.

Variables declared in explicit declarations are called
direct, since the declaration associates an identifier with
the variable, and the identifier is used to refer to the
variable.   In contrast, variables may be accessed
indirectly through a pointer variable.   An explicit
declaration of a pointer variable indicates the type of
variable to which it can point.   The pointer's value may be
assigned only to other pointer variables declared to point
to the same type.   It may also assume the value NIL, which
points to no variable.   Because pointer variables may also
occur as components of structured variables, the use of
pointers permits the representation of complex interconnected
data structures.

The most fundamental statement in PLZ is the assignment statement. It specifies that a newly computed value be assigned to a variable (or a component of a variable). The value is obtained by evaluating an expression. Expressions consist of variables, constants, operators, and procedures which return exactly one value. PLZ defines a fixed set of operators, each of which can be regarded as describing a mapping from the operand types into the result type. The set of operators is subdivided into groups of:

1. arithmetic operators--addition, subtraction, sign inversion, multiplication, integer division, computing the remainder. (MOD), absolute value (ABS), increment (INC), and decrement (DEC).

2. logical operators--negation (NOT), conjunction (AND), disjunction (OR), and exclusive or (XOR).

3. relational operators--equality, inequality, and ordering, which may appear only in if statements.

4. conditional operators--ANDIF and ORIF, which can be used where partial evaluation of conditional expressions is desired, and may appear only in if statements.

In order to allow a controlled breach of the type compatibility checking system, explicit type converters may be used as unary operators causing the value of the associated operand type to be converted to a value of the converter type. Type converters may be either standard or user-defined type identifiers.

The procedure statement causes the execution of the designated procedure and the assignment of any returned values (see below).

The return statement is used to terminate execution of the procedure in which it appears, and to continue execution following the procedure invocation in the calling procedure.

There are two kinds of loop control statements: the exit statement is used to terminate a loop, and the repeat statement is used to continue execution at the top of the loop. Both of these statements may be qualified by a loop identifier which allows multiple-level control of execution with respect to nested loop statements.

Assignment, procedure, return and loop control statements
are referred to as simple statements. Structured
statements specify conditional, selective, or repeated
execution of their components; a component of a structured
statement is a sequence of simple and/or structured
statements. Sequential execution of simple or structured
statements is implied by their sequence in the program
text.

Conditional or selective execution is controlled by the if
statement and the select statement. The if statement
serves to make the execution of a component dependent on
the value of an expression; the select statement allows
for the selection among many components according to the
value of a selector. Thus, the select statement is a
natural extension of the if statement. Repeated execution
is controlled by the loop statement.

2.2 THE CONSTRUCTION OF A PROGRAM

A program consists of one or more separately compiled
modules which serve to define the scope of data and
action statements and permit the combination of portions
of a program written in different members of the PLZ family
of languages.

A group of statements (including both action and data
statements) defining an executable portion of a module may
be named by an identifier and is then called a procedure,
and its declaration is called a procedure declaration. A
variable which is not declared LOCAL in a given procedure
body and is not a parameter to that procedure is accessible
in that body only if it is accessible in the scope of the
module containing the procedure body. A variable is
accessible throughout a module only if:

> 1) it is explicitly declared in a GLOBAL or
>   INTERNAL declaration, or
>
> 2) it is explicitly imported into the given
>   module by an EXTERNAL declaration.

A procedure has a fixed number of parameters, each of which
is denoted within the procedure heading by an identifier
called the formal parameter, which is considered local to
the procedure body. Upon an invocation of the procedure
statement, an actual quantity must be indicated for each
parameter which can be referenced from within the procedure
through the formal parameter. This quantity is called the
actual parameter. Parameters are passed to procedures by
value only. An actual parameter is an expression which is
evaluated once. The formal parameter represents a local
variable whose value is the result of this evaluation.
Thus, a call by reference can be achieved only by passing a
pointer to a variable.

A procedure may return one or more values; the values to be
returned are the values (at the time of return from the
procedure) of the variables declared in the RETURNS portion
of the procedure heading. These variables are also
considered local to the procedure body, but unlike the
formal parameters, their values are undefined upon
procedure entry. Thus, some explicit assignment of values
to these variables must appear within the procedure body
for the returned values to be meaningful.

Variables and procedures must be associated with exactly one
of the following declaration classes: GLOBAL, EXTERNAL,
INTERNAL, or LOCAL. GLOBAL specifies that the variable is
defined in the current module, and may be used in other
modules as well. EXTERNAL specifies that the variable is
used in the current module, but defined in another module.
INTERNAL specifies that the variable is defined in the current
module and cannot be used in other modules. LOCAL specifies
that the variable can be accessed only inside the procedure
in which it is declared. Of these four classes, EXTERNAL,
GLOBAL and INTERNAL can be used only to declare variables
at the module level; LOCAL can be used only to declare
variables at the procedure level. Procedure declarations
must be either GLOBAL, INTERNAL or EXTERNAL, with access
by other modules in a manner analogous to variables.

Constant identifiers are defined using the CONSTANT class,
and can be defined only at the module level. Thus, the
scope of a constant identifier is the module scope, and it
cannot be used outside the module unless it is redefined.

Type identifiers are defined using the TYPE class; they can
be defined only at the module level and are valid type
definitions only within the scope of the module.

PLZ has been designed to permit one-pass translation. To
this end, identifiers must be declared before they are used.

The PLZ/SYS language has intentionally been designed to not
include any specific Input/Output statements; instead, a
program may invoke other PLZ procedures which actually
perform the desired I/O. These procedures might be provided
by the system in which the PLZ program is executed, or they
might be provided by the user.

Example:

```
bubble_sort MODULE

CONSTANT
   false := 0
   true := 1

EXTERNAL
   printarray PROCEDURE (first ↑WORD count BYTE)

INTERNAL
   a ARRAY [10 WORD]
      := [33   10   2000   400     410
           3    3     33   500   1999]

   sort PROCEDURE (n BYTE)
      LOCAL
         i   j   limit BYTE
         temp WORD
         switched BYTE

      ENTRY
      DO
         switched := false
         i := 0
         limit := n-2
         DO
            IF i > limit THEN EXIT FI
            j := i + 1
            IF a[i] > a[j] THEN
                  switched := true
                  temp := a[i]
                  a[i] := a[j]
                  a[j] := temp
            FI
            i += 1
         OD
         IF switched = false THEN RETURN FI
      OD
      END sort

GLOBAL
   main PROCEDURE
      ENTRY
         sort (10)
         printarray(#a[0] 10)
      END main

END bubble_sort
```

3. NOTATION, TERMINOLOGY, AND VOCABULARY

The syntax is described in a modification of Backus-Naur
form, in which syntactic constructs are denoted by lower-
case English words or phrases not enclosed in any special
marks. These words also suggest the nature or meaning of
the construct, and are used in the accompanying description
of semantics. Basic symbols of the language are either
written in upper case (for keywords) or enclosed in quote
marks (for symbols); e.g., PROCEDURE and '+'. Possible
repetition of a construct is indicated by appending the
construct with either a + to signify 1 or more repetitions
or a * to signify 0 or more repetitions. Parentheses are
metasymbols used to enclose a group of constructs to be
followed by a repetition symbol. Possible omission of a
construct is indicated by enclosing the construct within
metasymbols [and]. The metasymbol | is used to signify
that one of several constructs may be selected, e.g., A|B
means that either A or B may be specified.

A descriptive grammar defining the syntax of PLZ is
distributed throughout this report; occasionally,
simplifications are made in the interests of clarity of
presentation. For convenient reference, the complete grammar
has been collected in the Appendix.

3.1 VOCABULARY

The primitive vocabulary of PLZ consists of basic symbols
classified into letters, digits, and special symbols. This
vocabulary is not the character set; the character set is
implementation dependent, and each implementation must
define, in its character set, distinct representations for
all the basic symbols. Notice that a particular
implementation need define only one character set (in
general, at least 64-character ASCII).

The basic symbols are:

```
letter          => 'A' | 'B' | ... | 'Z'
                => 'a' | 'b' | ... | 'z'

digit           => '0' | '1' | '2' | '3' | '4'
                => '5' | '6' | '7' | '8' | '9'

hex_digit       => digit
                => 'A' | 'B' | 'C' | 'D' | 'E' | 'F'
                => 'a' | 'b' | 'c' | 'd' | 'e' | 'f'

special_symbol  => '+' | '-' | '*' | '/' | '='
                => '<' | '>' | '<=' | '>=' | '<>'
                => '.' | '&' | '↑' | ':=' | '#'
                => '[' | ']' | '(' | ')' | '+='
                => '-=' | '?' | '...'
```

```
word_symbol        => ABS | AND | ANDIF | ARRAY
                   => BYTE | CASE | CONSTANT | DEC
                   => DO | ELSE | END | ENTRY | EXIT
                   => EXTERNAL | FI | FROM | GLOBAL
                   => IF | INC | INTEGER | INTERNAL
                   => LOCAL | MOD | MODULE | NIL
                   => NOT | OD | OR | ORIF | PROCEDURE
                   => RECORD | REPEAT | RETURN | RETURNS
                   => SHORT_INTEGER | SIZEOF | THEN
                   => TYPE T WORD | XOR

delimiter          => ',' | ';' | ':' |   space
                   => tab  |  formfeed  |   linefeed
                   => carriage_return
```

The construct

   '!' any_sequence_of_symbols_not_containing_! '!'

may be inserted anywhere that a delimiter may appear (see
3.2). It is called a comment and is treated as a single
delimiter.

3.2 LEXICAL STRUCTURE

The primitive lexical unit of PLZ is called a token. A
token is either a special_symbol or word_symbol of the
vocabulary, an identifier, or a literal constant (see
section 4). The text of a program is built up out of
declarations and statements, which are in turn built up of
tokens according to the syntax specified below. In general,
tokens are delimited by separators. The syntax is constructed
in such a way that a token may always be legally followed
by one or more separators.

Delimiters and special_symbols are collectively referred to
as separators. The distinction between delimiters and
special_symbols is that the special_symbols have semantic
significance (for example, the symbols '(', ')' and '[',
']' serve to enclose parameter lists and array indices,
respectively), whereas delimiters have no meaning other
than as separators of tokens. The class of delimiters
includes spaces, tabs, carriage returns, commas, colons,
semicolons, and comments. Aside from the requirement
that at least one separator must appear between two
word_symbols or identifiers, PLZ requires no punctuation
between declarations and/or statements. This may be
interpreted to mean that the user may utilize punctuation
such as semicolons, colons or commas however he wishes to
improve readability.

```
PLZ_text              => separator* [id_constant_text]
                            (separator+ id_constant_text)*

id_constant_text      => identifier
                      => word_symbol
                      => literal_constant

separator             => delimiter_text
                      => special_symbol
```

There are several kinds of brackets which are used to group
statements for various purposes. The following list gives
the unique closing bracket for each opening bracket.

```
IF            FI
DO            OD
PROCEDURE     END
MODULE        END
```

4. IDENTIFIERS AND LITERAL CONSTANTS

Identifiers serve to denote constants, variables, loop
names, and procedures. Their association must be unique
within their scope of validity; i.e., within the scope in
which they are declared (see 6, 7.4).

Each time an identifier is used, it must be written in
exactly the same way (i.e., with the same capitalization)
as it was written when it was declared.

     identifier   => letter (letter | digit | '_')*

The usual decimal notation is used for numbers, which are
the literal constants of the data types BYTE, WORD,
SHORT_INTEGER and INTEGER. Numbers may also be written in
hexadecimal notation. Note that numbers are always
written without a sign; a negative constant can be
written as an expression, e.g., -14.

     number   => integer
                      => hex_number

     integer   => digit+

     hex_number   => '%' hex_digit+

A sequence of one or more characters enclosed by single quote
marks is called a character_sequence. Each character
represents an 8-bit quantity that may be manipulated as a
BYTE or SHORT_INTEGER data type whose value is dependent on
the underlying character set. A character, whether or not
it is in the printing character set, can also be represented
in a character_sequence as follows:

     %hh

where each h stands for a hexadecimal digit and
represents the character code with the hexadecimal
representation hh.

For convenience, %L, %T, %R, %P, %%, and %Q represent
linefeed, tab, carriage return, page (formfeed), %, and
single quote, respectively, within a character_sequence.

     character_sequence
                    => ''' character_text+ '''

     character_text => character
                    => special_character_text

```
character          => any_character_except_%_or_'

special_character_text
                   => '%' special_character
                   => '%' hex_digit hex_digit

special_character
                   => 'L' | 'T' | 'R' | 'P' | 'Q' | '%'
                   => 'l' | 't' | 'r' | 'p' | 'q'
```

Examples:

```
'A'
'Here is an ESC character:  %1B'
'First line%RSecond line%R'
'Quote%Qinside a quote%Q'
```

5. CONSTANTS

A constant is either a literal constant (such as a number
or a character_sequence), an identifier declared as a
constant, or an expression involving only constants. The
value of a constant expression must be computable at compile
time.

A constant represents a fixed value whose type is compatible
with one of the two disjoint classes of simple types:
arithmetic or pointer types. Numbers and character constants
(see 5.2) are only compatible with arithmetic types, which
include any type whose base type is INTEGER, WORD,
SHORT_INTEGER, or BYTE. The literal NIL is a value which
is only compatible with pointer types (see 6.3).

The rules for constructing constant expressions are similar
to those for general arithmetic expressions (see section 8
for a description of the various operators).

```
        constant_expression  => constant_term
                                   (add_op constant_term)*

        constant_term         => constant_factor
                                   (mult_op constant_factor)*

        constant_factor       => unary_op constant_factor
                              => constant
                              => '(' constant_expression ')'

        constant              => number
                              => character_constant
                              => constant_identifier
                              => SIZEOF static_variable
                              => SIZEOF type_identifier
                              => SIZEOF constant_identifier
```

Examples:

```
        16
        'A' OR $80
        'This is a character_sequence'
        (BUF_LENGTH+1)/2
```

5.1 CONSTANT DEFINITIONS

A constant definition introduces an identifier as a synonym
to a constant value. The value to be assigned to the constant
identifier is the value of a constant expression; all constant
identifiers appearing in the expression must have been
previously defined.

Constants are defined at the module level and thus have the
module as their scope. Constant definitions which
are to be used within the scope of more than one module
must have their complete definition in each module.

The general form of a constant definition is

        identifier ':=' constant_expression

Examples:

    CONSTANT

        REC_LENGTH   := 64
        BUF_LENGTH   := 4*REC_LENGTH
        SEMICOLON   := ';'
        BIGNUM   := 65000
        SMALLNUM   := -1

5.2   CHARACTER AND TEXT CONSTANTS

A character constant is a character_sequence of one or two
characters whose value can be represented either by a constant
identifier or by a variable of arithmetic type only. For
example, 'A' can be assigned to either a BYTE or a WORD
variable, while 'AB' can be assigned to a WORD. The order of
bytes in character constants longer than 8 bits is
implementation dependent, and thus the use of multiple-byte
character constants should be avoided.

A text constant is a character_sequence of one or more
characters that can be represented by a one-dimensional array
of 8-bit values (see 5.3 and 7.2.1).

        character_constant
                        => ''' character_text [character_text] '''

        text_constant   => character_sequence

5.3 ADDRESS CONSTANTS

An address constant is a pointer value which the compiler
can calculate based on its knowledge of the allocation of
variables, and is either used either to initialize a pointer
variable when it is declared, or can be assigned to an
appropriate pointer variable during program execution. An
address constant evaluates to the address of a variable of
any type including structured types.

One form of an address constant is

>   '#' static_variable

where static_variable is either a variable of any simple type,
an array or record identifier (in which case the first memory
location of the structure is used), or a particular array
element or record field. The only restriction is that the
static_variable has an address which can be calculated
at compile-time, thus prohibiting variable indices in an
array, pointer operators, procedure invocations, etc.

The other form of an address constant is

>   '#' text_constant

where the value is a pointer to the first element of an
unnamed, one-dimensional array of 8-bit values initialized
to the character values in the text_constant. This is
similar to the explicit declaration of an array of unspecified
length (see 7.2.1) except the array has no associated
identifier, and the type of the array element is compatible
with any variable whose base type is BYTE or SHORT_INTEGER
(see 8.1.2).

Examples:

>   #ROOT
>   #A[10]
>   #PATIENT.NAME
>   #'PROGRAM ABORT%R'

6. DATA TYPES

A data type determines the set of values which variables of that type may assume and the set of basic operations that may be performed on them.

A type definition associates an identifier with a type. A type must be either one of the five predefined simple types (BYTE, WORD, INTEGER, SHORT_INTEGER, and pointer), one of the two structured types (ARRAY and RECORD), or the name of a previously defined type. Thus, type identifiers must be declared before they are used; recursive or mutually recursive types (i.e., types which contain themselves as components, or types which reference each other) are not permitted. This restriction is relaxed in the case of pointers, so that the type to which a pointer is bound may remain undeclared until the pointer is used in some denotation (see 7.2.3). This allows, for instance, records which contain pointers to records of the same type.

Sometimes it is neither necessary nor desirable to associate an identifier with a type. For such cases, PLZ allows the user to define the type directly in the variable declaration (see section 7). Notice that structures declared in this way cannot contain pointers to structures of the same type, since there is no name for the type.

Internally, a base type is associated with every type. The base type is implicit in every type definition; it is the standard type which the defined type ultimately represents. For example, in the sequence of definitions:

```
TYPE
        CHAR BYTE
        STR_CHAR CHAR
```

the base type of both CHAR and STR_CHAR is BYTE. Thus, the base type provides the information necessary to determine the set of basic operations that can be performed on a defined type. The fundamental difference between the defined type and the base type is that the defined type, not the base type, is used to determine type compatibility in expressions, assignments, and actual/formal parameter correspondence for procedures.

Types are defined at the module level and thus have the module as their scope. Type definitions that are to be used within the scope of more than one module must have their complete definition in each module.

The identifiers which appear as field names of a record type are considered local to that record type (and not to the scope in which the record type is defined), in the sense that the same identifier name may appear (possibly in different positions) in other record type definitions, and even in the enclosing scope of the record type definition.

- 21 -

6.1 SIMPLE TYPES

The following simple types are standard in PLZ and may be
used in all programs.

WORD   a 16-bit quantity whose values are
                        the non-negative integers in the
                        range 0 to 65535.

BYTE   an 8-bit quantity whose values are
                        the non-negative integers in the
                        range 0 to 255. This value may
                        also be the representation of a
                        single character from the character
                        set.

INTEGER   a 16-bit quantity whose values represent
                        the positive and negative integers in
                        the range -32768 to 32767.

SHORT_INTEGER   an 8-bit quantity whose values represent
                        the positive and negative integers in the
                        range -128 to 127. This value
                        may also be the representation of
                        a single character from the
                        character set.

pointer (↑)   a machine-dependent quantity whose value
                        represents a memory address (see 6.3).

6.2 STRUCTURED TYPES

A structured type is characterized by the type(s) of its
components and by the structuring method.

6.2.1 ARRAY TYPES

An array type is a structure consisting of a fixed number
of components which are all of the same type, called the
component type. The elements of the array are designated
by indices whose values belong to one of the simple base
types WORD, INTEGER, BYTE or SHORT_INTEGER. The array
type definition specifies the component type and the
number and maximum value of each of the indices, and
associates an identifier with the type. Each index ranges
from the value 0 to one less than the maximum indicated in
the declaration. For example, an array with 10 elements
may be indexed from 0 to 9. Each index value in the
definition must be specified as a constant expression;
thus, variable upper bounds are not permitted. The array
type definition does not specify (either implicitly or
explicitly) the type of the index and thus the same array
may be indexed by values of either WORD, INTEGER, BYTE,
or SHORT_INTEGER base type.

    array_type_definition => identifier array_type

    array_type => ARRAY '[' constant_expression+ type ']'
                => array_type_identifier

Examples:

        TYPE
                BUFFER ARRAY [128 BYTE]
                TABLE ARRAY [256 WORD]
                MATRIX ARRAY [100 100 BYTE]
                TABLE_COPY TABLE

6.2.2 RECORD TYPES

A record type is a structure consisting of a fixed number
of components called fields. Unlike the array, components
are not constrained to be of identical type and are
accessed, not by an index, but by a field identifier. The
record type definition specifies a type and an identifier
for each component, and associates an identifier with the
record structure itself. The scope of these field
identifiers is the record definition itself. As for all
types, there are two ways to declare a record type: in a
record type definition (in which an identifier is
associated with the record structure), or in a record
variable declaration (in which an identifier is associated
with an instance or collection of instances; e.g., arrays
of records) of the record structure. In the latter case,
the declaration cannot include an identifier for the
structure itself, so that records declared in this way
cannot have fields which are pointers to themselves.

```
    record_type_definition  => identifier record_type

    record_type             => RECORD '[' field_declaration+ ']'
                            => record_type_identifier

    field_declaration       => identifier+ type
```

Examples:

```
        TYPE
                PATIENT RECORD [AGE, HEIGHT, WEIGHT BYTE
                                BIRTH RECORD [DAY, MO, YR BYTE]
                                SEX BYTE
                                ROOM WORD
                                ]
                MSG RECORD [LENGTH BYTE
                            CHAR ARRAY [50 BYTE]
                            ]
                TITLE MSG
```

6.3 POINTER TYPES

Any variable may be referred to directly by its identifier;
any use of the variable through its associated identifer is
thus called a direct reference. In contrast, variables may
also be accessed indirectly via a pointer value which is
contained in a variable declared to be a pointer to a
particular type. The values of a pointer variable can thus
only be addresses of other variables of the type specified
in the declaration. A pointer variable may be used to point
to any type of variable, including all the simple types as
well as arrays, records and other pointers.

The pointer value NIL belongs to every pointer type, and
points to no variable at all.

          pointer_type_definition => identifier pointer_type

          pointer_type   => '↑' type
                                  => pointer_type_identifier

A pointer to a BYTE, WORD, INTEGER, SHORT_INTEGER, or
pointer (or to a user-defined type whose base type is one
of these types) is used to refer to any variable of the
declared type, including variables which are part of a
structure. For example,

          TYPE
                    PTRB ↑BYTE
                    CHAR BYTE
                    PTRC ↑CHAR
                    PTRB2 ↑↑BYTE
                    A ARRAY [10 BYTE]
                    B ARRAY [10 BYTE]

In this example, any variable of type PTRB can be used to
point to a variable of type BYTE, for instance, an element
of any array of type A or type B. Any variable of type
PTRC can be used to point to a variable of type CHAR (the
defined type), but it cannot be used to point to any
variable of type BYTE (the base type). A variable of type
PTRB2 can be used to point to any variable that has itself
been declared as a pointer to type BYTE. For example, with
the following variable declaration,

          INTERNAL
                    BYTEPTR ↑BYTE

A variable of type PTRB2 can point to BYTEPTR, but not to a
variable of type PTRB, which is a different type from
'↑BYTE'.

A pointer to a structure is declared by using the type
identifier of the structure. It is used as a pointer to
the base address (first memory location) of an instance of
that structure. It cannot be used to point to an element
of the structure. Continuing the above example,

```
TYPE
        PTRA ↑A
        R RECORD [F1, F2 BYTE
                  F3 WORD
                  F4 CHAR]
        S RECORD [F1, F2 BYTE
                  F3 WORD
                  F4 CHAR]
        PTRR ↑R
```

A variable of type PTRA can point only to arrays that are
declared to be of type A, and thus cannot point to any
other type of array, including arrays of type B whose
declaration looks identical to A. Similarly, a variable of
type PTRR can point only to records that are declared to
be of type R, and thus cannot point to any other type of
record, including records of type S whose declaration looks
identical to R. (See section 7.3 for a discussion on how
to use these pointers to access elements of the structure
to which they point.)

6.4 TYPE COMPATIBILITY

The general rule throughout PLZ concerning data values is
that only variables with compatible types may appear
together in expressions, assignments, and actual/formal
parameter bindings in procedure invocations. Mixing
variables of different defined types causes an error. (See
8.1.3 for a mechanism to convert data types).

Two variables of simple types (not including pointers) are
said to have compatible types only if their defined types
are identical. That is, the types appearing in the
declaration of each variable must be the same identifiers,
regardless of whether the type is one of the standard types
BYTE, SHORT_INTEGER, WORD, INTEGER, or a user-defined
type whose base type is one of the standard simple types.

Example:

```
    TYPE
            CHAR      BYTE
    INTERNAL
            A,B       BYTE
            C         CHAR
            D         BYTE
            E         WORD
```

Here A, B and D are all compatible, while C and E are
incompatible with any of the others.

Two variables of structured types (array or record) are said to have compatible types only if either they appear in the same declaration list, or their declarations use the same user-defined type identifier. That is, each time a structured type is explicitly described within a module, a unique type is defined.

Example:

```
        TYPE
                BUFFER ARRAY [128 BYTE]
                DATE RECORD [DAY MONTH YEAR BYTE]
        INTERNAL
                A,B     BUFFER
                C,D     ARRAY [128 BYTE]
                E       BUFFER
                F       ARRAY [128 BYTE]
                G       DATE
                H       DATE
                I,J     RECORD [DAY MONTH YEAR BYTE]
                K       RECORD [DAY MONTH YEAR BYTE]
```

Here A, B and E are compatible; C and D are compatible; G and H are compatible; I and J are compatible; F and K are incompatible with any of the others.

Two pointer variables are compatible only if the
declaration of the objects pointed to are compatible, that
is, after replacing each '↑' operator with the textual
declaration for the objects pointed to, the resulting
types are compatible. This allows pointers to be bound only
to objects of a specific type, thus inhibiting modifications
to data values at arbitrary memory addresses.

Example:

```
TYPE
     BUFFER ARRAY [128 BYTE]
     STRING ↑BYTE
INTERNAL
     BUF     BUFFER
     A,B     STRING
     C,D     ↑BYTE
     E       STRING
     F       ↑BYTE
     G       ↑BUFFER
     H       ↑BUFFER
     I       ↑ARRAY [128 BYTE]
     J       ↑ARRAY [128 BYTE]
     K       ↑STRING
```

Here A, B and E are compatible; C, D and F are
compatible; G and H are compatible; I and J are not only
incompatible, but because each occurrence of a structured
type is considered a unique type, they are useless since
there is no way to create a type-compatible structure to
which they can point; K is incompatible with any of the
others but is nonetheless useful as illustrated below. The
following assignments are allowed (see 7.3, 8.1.2, and
9.1.1):

```
A      :=  #BUF[3]
C      :=  #BUF[3]
A↑     :=  C↑
G      :=  #BUF
A↑     :=  G↑[3]
K      :=  #A
E      :=  K↑
C↑     :=  K↑↑
```

7. DECLARATION AND DENOTATION OF VARIABLES

A variable declaration associates an identifier with a
variable of that type. It consists of a list of
identifiers denoting the variables, followed by their type
and optional initialization. An initialization value must
be type-compatible with the associated variable. The
initialization is similar to an assignment statement executed
immediately after the PLZ program is loaded into memory,
except no program code is generated. This implies that, after
execution, a program must either reinitialize its variables
or be reloaded before being executed again. EXTERNAL and
LOCAL variables cannot be initialized.

There are several rules and special symbols used for
initializations in general. When a single declaration
contains more than one variable identifier, the corresponding
initialization values are listed within square brackets. A
simple variable is initialized using a value which must be
determinable at compile time. A structured variable is
initialized using a "constructor", which is simply a list of
values enclosed by square brackets, with each level of
nesting within the structure denoted by a matching set of
brackets. A special symbol, '...', indicates that the
immediately preceding value or constructor is to be repeated
for the rest of the variables at the current level of nesting.
The special symbol '?' can be used as a placeholder in a list
of initial values for simple variables or components of
simple type within a structure, and indicates that the
corresponding simple variable remains unassigned. An empty
constructor, '[]', indicates that the corresponding
structured variable remains unassigned.

Variable identifiers must be declared before they are
used. Denotations of variables either designate a simple
variable, a component of a structured variable, or a
variable referenced by a pointer.

7.1 SIMPLE VARIABLES

Simple variables are variables whose base type is one of
the simple types. The declaration of a GLOBAL or INTERNAL
simple variable may optionally initialize the variable.
There are two ways to initialize simple variables: with a
single constant value if there is only one variable identifier,
or with a list of constants enclosed in square brackets if
there is more than one variable identifier in a single
declaration. In the second case, the variables are initialized
in left to right order from the initial list. (Having fewer
constants than variables is permitted, but having more is
flagged as an error.)

```
simple_variable_declaration
                    => identifier simple_type
                       [ ':=' initial_value ]
                    => identifier identifier+ simple_type
                       [ ':=' '[' initial_value*
                                              ['...'] ']' ]

initial_value       => type_converter initial_value
                    => (INC|DEC) initial_value
                    => constant_expression
                    => '#' static_variable
                    => '#' text_constant
                    => NIL
                    => '?'
```

A simple variable is denoted by the identifier appearing in its declaration.

Examples:

```
TYPE
        COLOR BYTE
INTERNAL
        HUE COLOR
        LIMIT WORD := %FFFF
        SUBTOTAL, TOTAL INTEGER := [0...]
        A,B,C BYTE := ['A', 'B', 'C']
```


7.2 STRUCTURED VARIABLES

A structured variable is a variable whose base type is one of the structured types. The variable type may be represented either by a type identifier which has already been associated with a structure via a type definition, or by specifying the structure in the structured variable declaration itself.

A component of a structured variable is denoted by the variable identifier followed by a selector specifying the component. The form of the selector depends on the structuring type of the variable.

7.2.1 INDEXED VARIABLES

An indexed variable is a variable whose base type is ARRAY.
Several array identifiers may appear in a single declaration,
and may optionally be initialized if declared GLOBAL or
INTERNAL. Each array component is initialized in left to
right order from the values given in the initial list, and
in row major form (i.e., the right-most subscript varies
fastest). There are two ways to initialize an array: with
a single constructor if there is only one array identifier,
or with a list of constructors enclosed in square brackets
if there is more than one array identifier in a single
declaration. In the first case, for a constructor containing
N elements, the first N components of the array taken in row-
major order are initialized. (Having more constants than the
number of array elements is flagged as an error.) In the
second case, the elements of each array are initialized to
the specified values within the corresponding constructor in
a manner similar to the first case.

For one-dimensional array initializations where the
component is a simple type, PLZ allows the length of the
array to be unspecified (by writing '*' for the index value
in the declaration), so that the length of the array is
determined by the number of elements in the initialization
list. When '*' is used, there are two ways to initialize
the array: with a list of constants enclosed in square
brackets or with a list of text_constants. In the second
case, the array component type must have an 8-bit base type
(BYTE or SHORT_INTEGER), and each byte of the array is
initialized to a single character value; the characters are
taken in left to right order from the sequence of
text_constants and put into the array in ascending memory
locations. For instance:

        ALPHA ARRAY [* BYTE] := 'ABCDEFGHIJKLMNOPQRSTUVWXYZ'

could be written:

        ALPHA ARRAY [* BYTE] := 'ABCDEFGHIJKLM'
                                'NOPQRSTUVWXYZ'

A unary operator, called SIZEOF, can be given the name of
an array variable or array type identifier as its argument
and produces a constant value which is the number of bytes
in the array (see 8.1.2).

```
array_variable_declaration
            => Identifier array_type
                 [ ':=' constructor ]
            => identifier identifier+ array_type
                 [ ':=' '[' constructor* ['...'] ']' ]
            => identifier ARRAY '[' '*' simple_type ']'
                 ':=' '[' initial_value+ ']'
            => identifier ARRAY '[' '*' simple_type ']'
                 ':=' text_constant+

  constructor => '[' initial_component* ['...'] ']'

  initial_component
            => initial_value
            => constructor
```

In the following examples, the array type is specified in
the variable declaration, instead of defining the arrays as
types:

```
    INTERNAL
            ONEDIM1, ONEDIM2 ARRAY [2 BYTE] := [[1...][2...]]
            TWODIM ARRAY [4 ARRAY [2 WORD]] := [[0...]...]
            MESSAGE ARRAY [* BYTE] := 'THIS IS A MESSAGE'
                (sizeof=17)
            ONEDIM3 ARRAY [* INTEGER] := [25535,0,(-4)]
                (sizeof=6)
            THREEDIM ARRAY [3 2 3 SHORT_INTEGER]
```

The following examples declare variables by specifying the
type as a user-defined type.

```
    TYPE
            BUFFER ARRAY [128 BYTE]
            MATRIX ARRAY [8 8 BYTE]

    INTERNAL
            CHARBUF BUFFER := [' '...]
            CHESSBOARD MATRIX
```

A component of an array variable is denoted by the variable
followed by a list of indices.

```
array_variable   => array_designator '[' array_index+ ']'

array_designator => array_identifier
                 => pointer_variable
                 => record_variable
                 => array_variable

array_index      => arithmetic_expression
```

The base type of each index in the list must be WORD,
INTEGER, BYTE or SHORT_INTEGER. Notice that the component
of an array of arrays (e.g., TWODIM[I]) is itself an array.
The indices of an array must conform with its declaration,
so that neither TWODIM[I,J] nor MATRIX[1][2] are valid with
the above declarations.

Some valid array denotations are:

```
CHARBUF[10]
CHESSBOARD[ROW COLUMN]
TWODIM[I][J]
```


7.2.2 RECORD VARIABLES AND FIELD DESIGNATORS

A record variable is a variable whose base type is RECORD.
Several record identifiers may appear in a single
declaration, and may optionally be initialized if declared
GLOBAL or INTERNAL. Each record field is initialized in
left to right order from the values given in the initial
list. There are two ways to initialize a record: with a
single constructor if there is only one record identifier,
or with a list of constructors enclosed in square brackets
if there is more than one record identifier in a single
declaration. In the first case, for a constructor containing
N elements, the first N fields are initialized. (Having more
constants than the number of record fields is flagged as an
error.) In the second case, the elements of each record are
initialized to the specified values within the corresponding
constructor in a manner similar to the first case. The
declaration of a record variable may either use a record type
identifier as the type, or may instead define the record
template in the record variable declaration itself.

```
record_variable_declaration
                 => identifier record_type
                    [ ':=' constructor ]
                 => identifier identifier+ record_type
                    [ ':=' '[' constructor* ['...'] ']' ]
```

A component (field) of a record variable is denoted by an expression called a field designator. The field designator consists of the record designator (which specifies the particular record being accessed) and a field identifier (which specifies which field is being accessed).

```
    record_variable      => record_designator
                                '.' field_identifier

    record_designator     => record_identifier
                          => pointer_variable
                          => array_variable
                          => record_variable
```

Examples:

```
    TYPE
      PATIENT RECORD [AGE, HEIGHT, WEIGHT BYTE
                      BIRTH RECORD [DAY, MO, YR BYTE]
                      SEX BYTE
                      ROOM WORD
                      ]

    INTERNAL
      FEMALE ARRAY [100 PATIENT] := [[?,?,?,[],'F']...]
            (only the SEX field of each record is initialized)
      DEAN, PROVOST PATIENT
      PROGRAMSTATUS RECORD [FLAGS BYTE
                            PROGRAM_COUNTER WORD] := [%80,0]
```

Some valid record denotations are:

```
    DEAN.ROOM
    PROVOST.BIRTH.YR
    FEMALE[I].BIRTH.DAY
    PROGRAMSTATUS.FLAGS
```

7.3 REFERENCED VARIABLES

Referenced variables are variables which are pointed to by some pointer variable. The base type of a pointer variable is type pointer. The defined type of a pointer variable is a combination of the number of levels of indirection (i.e., the number of '↑' appearing in the declaration), along with the defined type to which it is declared to point (see 6.3).

A pointer to a component of a structure is declared by specifying that the pointer points to the type of the desired component. Thus, the pointer variable is not restricted to point only within the array or record; rather, it can point to any variable of the specified type. In contrast, a pointer to a record or an array structure itself is declared by specifying the record or array type. Such a pointer is restricted to point to the beginning of any record or array of the specified type. Thus the compiler can ensure that any field references (for records) or indices (for arrays) are computed from the base address.

The only operations defined on pointers are the tests for equality and ordering (based on the underlying machine-dependent addressing scheme), the pointer operator '↑' (which yields the variable referred to by the pointer), the address operator '#' which yields the address of the pointer variable, and the INC and DEC operators (which yield a pointer to the next and previous values in memory of the type pointed to).

A pointer variable is declared as a simple variable (see 7.1) and may be initialized with a type-compatible value. If p is a pointer variable which points to data type T, p denotes that variable and its pointer value, whereas p↑ denotes the variable of type T referenced by p. If p involves more than one level of indirection, then to get the value to which p ultimately points, as many '↑' as appear in the declaration of p must be appended to p.

```
pointer_variable      => pointer_designator '↑'

pointer_designator    => pointer_identifier
                      => array_variable
                      => record_variable
                      => pointer_variable
```

For example, the following set of declarations form a
structure for a hash table. HASH_PTR points to some
"bucket" (i.e., an element of SYM_BUCKETS) where a bucket
is the head of a linked list of names which hash to that
bucket. Each element of SYM_BUCKETS points to the head of
a list of TABLE_ENTRYs in the array SYMBOL_TABLE. Given a
bucket by the hash function, searching down the linked list
of names for a given name is accomplished via the NEXT
field of the record using the pointer variable TABLE_PTR.

        TYPE
                STRING RECORD [LENGTH BYTE
                              CHARS ↑BYTE]
                ENTRY_PTR ↑TABLE_ENTRY
                TABLE_ENTRY RECORD [NAME STRING
                                    NEXT ENTRY_PTR]
                STRPTR ↑STRING
                NAMES ARRAY [100 TABLE_ENTRY]
                BUCKETS ARRAY [100 ENTRY_PTR]

        INTERNAL
                CHARSTR STRING
                CHARSTR_PTR STRPTR
                SYMBOL_TABLE NAMES
                SYM_BUCKETS BUCKETS
                HASH_PTR ↑ENTRY_PTR
                TABLE_PTR ENTRY_PTR := NIL

Some valid variable denotations are:

                CHARSTR.LENGTH   (type = BYTE)
                CHARSTR_PTR↑.LENGTH   (type = BYTE)
                CHARSTR.CHARS↑   (type = BYTE)
                SYMBOL_TABLE[1].NAME.CHARS (type = ↑BYTE)
                SYM_BUCKETS[1]↑.NAME.CHARS (type = ↑BYTE)
                HASH_PTR↑   (type = ENTRY_PTR)
                HASH_PTR↑↑   (type = TABLE_ENTRY)

Notice that the variable designator CHARSTR_PTR↑ functions
semantically the same as CHARSTR, since they are both
record variables of type STRING. Similarly, for arrays and
pointers to arrays, the pointer can be used to index into
the array. For example, with the declaration:

```
        INTERNAL
                SYM_LENGTH BYTE
                SYM_TAB_PTR ↑NAMES
```

Some valid assignments and expressions are:

```
                SYM_TAB_PTR := # SYMBOL_TABLE
                SYM_LENGTH := SYM_TAB_PTR↑[10].NAME.LENGTH
                SYM_LENGTH := SYMBOL_TABLE[10].NAME.LENGTH
```

The last two assignments are equivalent. The first
assignment exemplifies the only way in which pointers to
arrays can be assigned initial values other than NIL.
Note that the array variable identifier must be given
without an index in this case.

7.4 SCOPE RULES

A "scope" is a region of text in which an identifier is known
with a single meaning. A scope is either

>   a module definition, bracketed by MODULE and the
>   matching END, or

>   a procedure declaration (see section 10), bracketed
>   by PROCEDURE and the matching END, or

>   a record definition, bracketed by '[' and the
>   matching ']'.

Note that procedure declarations are not allowed within
other procedure declarations so that in any module there
can be at most three nested levels of scoping: module
level, procedure level, and record level for records
declared in procedures.

A variable identifier is accessible in a scope S if it is

>   declared in S or in the scope of the module
>   or procedure definition containing S, or

>   declared EXTERNAL in the module definition
>   containing S, or

>   explicitly imported into S through a formal
>   parameter of the procedure declaration in
>   which S appears.

New identifiers are declared

      in a variable, procedure, type or constant
      declaration in the module,

      as record components,

      as formal parameters, return parameters, or
      local variables of a procedure declaration, or

      as loop labels.

New identifiers are accessible within the newly established
scope. They are not accessible outside of this scope,
except that field identifiers of records are accessible
outside the scope when used in a field designator, which is
considered to be a continuation of that scope.

The name declared by a procedure declaration is considered
to be declared in the entire scope of the enclosing module
definition. The formal parameters of the procedure
declaration, if any, are accessible only in the scope of
the procedure.

A new identifier may not be introduced which is the same as
any other identifier introduced in the scope (notice that
record field identifiers may use identifier names appearing
in the scope outside the current level of record
definition).

An identifier used in a scope and not declared in that
scope is said to be free in that scope. Any identifier
which is free in the scope of a procedure must be declared
in the enclosing scope (i.e., the scope of the module).
Thus, procedures do not explicitly import variables, as
modules do via the EXTERNAL declaration.

A module scope has the property that all its possible
interactions with the rest of the program can be determined
by examining its import and export list (i.e., the variables
declared GLOBAL or EXTERNAL), and the parameters of GLOBAL
or EXTERNAL procedures (since parameters may be passed which
are pointers to variables in other modules' scopes).

The value of a variable can change only

> as the result of assignment to that variable
> or one of its components, either directly or
> indirectly (through a pointer to that variable),
> or
>
> as a result of a procedure call in which that variable
> was pointed to by an actual parameter corresponding
> to a formal parameter of type pointer, or
>
> as a result of a procedure call that has side-effects
> (i.e., the procedure modifies variables other than its
> own locals). If the variables modified by the
> procedure appear in the expression invoking the
> procedure, unexpected results may occur.

8. EXPRESSIONS

Expressions are constructs denoting rules of computation
for obtaining values of variables and generating new values
by the application of operators. Expressions may consist
of operands (i.e., variables, constants, and procedures
that return exactly one value of the appropriate type) and
operators. In addition to the conventional arithmetic
operators, several other operators are defined to facilitate
the construction of relational or conditional expressions
in the restricted context of an if statement (see section
9.2.1.1).

The rules of composition specify operator precedences
according to six classes of operators. The unary operators
have the highest precedence, then the multiplying operators,
then the adding operators, then the relational operators,
then ANDIF and finally, with the lowest precedence, ORIF.
Sequences of operators of the same precedence are executed
from left to right.

The rules of precedence are reflected by the following
syntax:

        conditional_expression => conditional_term
                                    (ORIF conditional_term)*

        conditional_term   => conditional_factor
                                    (ANDIF conditional_factor)*

        conditional_factor   => arithmetic_expression
                                    [rel_op arithmetic_expression]

        arithmetic_expression   => arithmetic_term
                                    (add_op arithmetic_term)*

        arithmetic_term   => arithmetic_factor
                                    (mult_op arithmetic_factor)*

        arithmetic_factor   => unary_operator
                                       arithmetic_factor
                                => constant
                                => variable
                                => '#' variable
                                => '#' text_constant
                                => NIL
                                => '(' conditional_expression ')'

        rel_op   => '=' | '<>' | '<' | '>'
                                => '<=' | '>='

```
add_op                  => '+' | '-' | OR | XOR

mult_op                 => '*' | '/' | MOD | AND

unary_operator          => unary_op | type_converter

unary_op                => '+' | '-' | ABS
                        => NOT | INC | DEC
```

Examples:

```
15
-X
A/B*C
T1[J] AND T2[J] XOR T3[J]
PTR↑.CHAR <> 'Y'
I > 10 ORIF A[I] = 0
```

The rules of precedence can be overridden since any expression enclosed within parentheses is evaluated independently from preceding or succeeding operators.

Examples:

```
2*3-4*5        = (2*3)-(4*5)         = -14
2*(3-4)*5      = ((2*(3-4))*5        = -10
60/10/2        = (60/10)/2           =   3
60/(10/2)                            =  12
4+7 AND 3      = 4+(7 AND 3)         =   7
(4+7) AND 3                          =   3
```

8.1 OPERATORS

The base types of the operands for each operator are given in the following tables along with the corresponding base type of the result. In accordance with the type compatibility conventions of PLZ, all operands must have the same defined type.

Arithmetic overflow during evaluation of an expression may be ignored.

8.1.1 BINARY OPERATORS

The three types of binary operators are:

    arithmetic operators
    logical operators
    relational operators

The arithmetic operators are valid only for operands whose
base type is one of the standard arithmetic types in PLZ,
namely those whose base type is WORD, BYTE, INTEGER, or
SHORT_INTEGER. The base type and defined type of the
result they produce is the same as the base type and
defined type, respectively, of the operands. The division
operator, /, truncates toward zero, so that -(A/B) =
-A/B = A/-B. The MOD operator is defined as A MOD B =
A-((A/B)*B), so that the sign of the result of MOD is
always the sign of the left operand. The right operand
of / or MOD must be non-zero, otherwise the result is
undefined. The symbols and operations of the arithmetic
operators are given in the following table.

                    ARITHMETIC OPERATORS

operator	operation
*	multiplication
/	division with truncation
MOD	modulus
+	addition
-	subtraction

The logical operators are valid for all types whose base
type is one of the standard arithmetic types in PLZ. The
result of the bitwise logical operation has the same base
type and defined type as the base type and defined type,
respectively, of the operands.

LOGICAL OPERATORS

operator	operations
AND	logical 'and'
OR	logical 'or'
XOR	logical 'exclusive or'

The relational operators are valid for all types whose
base type is one of the standard arithmetic types in PLZ,
as well as for all types whose base type is pointer.
The symbols and operations of the relational operators
are given in the following table. The comparisons are
signed or unsigned according to whether the operands are
signed or unsigned.

RELATIONAL OPERATORS

operator	operation
=	equal
<>	not equal
<	less than
>	greater than
<=	less than or equal
>=	greater than or equal

A relational operator may be used only in a conditional
expression that controls an if statement since a data
result is never generated.

8.1.2 UNARY OPERATORS

For the unary operators the base type and defined type of
the result is the same as the base type and defined type,
respectively, of the operand (except for type converters,
see 8.1.3).

UNARY OPERATORS

operator	operation	base type of operand
+	unary plus	arithmetic
-	unary minus	arithmetic
ABS	absolute value	arithmetic
NOT	logical complement	arithmetic
INC	the value of the pointer plus the length of the base type to which it points	pointer
DEC	the value of the pointer minus the length of the base type to which it points	pointer
SIZEOF	determine number of bytes of storage occupied by operand	any type (result is a constant value)
#	address of variable	any type (result has base type pointer)

The SIZEOF operator can be applied to any static variable
(see 5.3) or type or constant identifier and produces a
constant value which is the number of bytes of storage
occupied by the operand. This value is useful for
communicating with storage allocators or I/O procedures.

Examples:

        TYPE
            MATRIX ARRAY[8 4 WORD]
        INTERNAL
            CLARA ARRAY [* BYTE] := 'NETTE'
            DISKSTREAM RECORD [FILE_DESC WORD
                               POSITION WORD
                               BUFFER ARRAY [256 WORD]
                               ]
                .
                .
                .
            SIZEOF MATRIX/SIZEOF WORD   (value is 32)
            SIZEOF CLARA   (value is 5)
            SIZEOF DISKSTREAM.BUFFER   (value is 512)

The address operator '#' can be applied to any type of
variable, and produces a value which is equivalent to a
pointer to that type. If only an array identifier is
given, then the pointer value is an array pointer type;
however, if an index is also given, then the pointer
value is to the array component's type. The index
expression may be either constant or variable. If only
a record identifier is given, then the pointer value is
a record pointer type; however, if a field name is also
given, then the pointer value is to the record field's
type. If the variable is a pointer designator, then the
resulting pointer value has the type "pointer to the type
of the pointer designator". Thus '#' effectively cancels
a single pointer operator '↑'.

Examples:

```
TYPE
    Ary ARRAY [5 BYTE]
    Rec RECORD [Fl WORD  F2 ↑BYTE]

INTERNAL
    I       BYTE
    BUFFER  Ary
    R       Rec
    BUFPTR  ↑Ary
    ROOT    ↑Rec
      .
      .
      .
    #I            (pointer to BYTE)
    #BUFFER       (pointer to ARRAY Ary)
    #BUFFER[I]    (pointer to BYTE)
    #R            (pointer to RECORD Rec)
    #R.Fl         (pointer to WORD)
    #R.F2         (pointer to pointer to BYTE)
    #ROOT         (pointer to pointer to RECORD Rec)
    #ROOT↑.Fl     (pointer to WORD)
    #ROOT↑.F2     (pointer to pointer to BYTE)
    #ROOT↑.F2↑    (pointer to BYTE)
```

The address operator '#' can also be applied to a
text_constant (see 5.3) and produces a value which is
equivalent to a pointer to the sequence of 8-bit values.
This value is type-compatible with any pointer variable
which is defined to point to a variable whose base type is
BYTE or SHORT_INTEGER.

Examples:

```
TYPE
    CHAR  BYTE
    MESSAGE ↑CHAR
EXTERNAL
    PRINT PROCEDURE (↑BYTE)
    PUTMESSAGE PROCEDURE (MSG MESSAGE, SIZE WORD)
INTERNAL
    GREETINGS ↑BYTE
      .
      .
      .
    GREETINGS := #'HELLO%R'
    PRINT (GREETINGS)
    PUTMESSAGE (#'WHAT IS YOUR NAME?',18)
```

8.1.3 TYPE CONVERTERS

In recognition of the fact that controlled breaches of
the type system are sometimes necessary, PLZ provides a
class of unary operators called type converters. Type
converters may be either the standard type identifiers
BYTE, SHORT_INTEGER, WORD or INTEGER, or a user-defined
type identifier. The unary operator takes a value of its
operand type and produces a value of the converter type
after any necessary conversion of the machine representation
of the operand expression.

```
         type_converter      => BYTE
                              => WORD
                              => INTEGER
                              => SHORT_INTEGER
                              => type_identifier
```

The effects of type conversion on the machine representation
of the various simple types are given in the table below.

EFFECTS OF TYPE CONVERSION

Operand Base Type

Converter Base Type	byte	word	short integer	integer	pointer
byte	=	t	=	t	t
word	r	=	r	=	w
short integer	=	t	=	t	t
integer	r	=	s	=	w
pointer	r	r	s	r	=

```
    = :  no effect
    r :  argument is right-justified in a field of zero bits
    s :  argument's sign is  preserved (sign extension)
    t :  truncation, producing low order 8 bits only
    w :  truncation, producing low order 16 bits only
```

It is important to realize that the numeric interpretation
of a value's representation may change even though the bit
pattern itself is unchanged. For example, if an INTEGER is
converted to a WORD, the same bit pattern that was
interpreted as a two's complement signed number is now
interpreted as an unsigned positive number.

Examples:

```
INTERNAL
          SMALLNUM   SHORT_INTEGER
          COUNT      INTEGER
          INDEX      WORD
             .
             .
             .
          COUNT := INTEGER SMALLNUM
          INDEX := WORD (COUNT + 1)
```

Because the normal type-checking mechanism of the compiler
is inhibited when type conversion is used, unexpected
results may occur when a value with a differing machine
representation is bound to a variable. This is
particularly true when mixing pointer and non-pointer
variables, since a pointer is necessarily a machine-
dependent value. Good programming practice suggests
that the effect of type conversion should be kept
localized by not passing type-converted values across
procedure or module boundaries if possible.

Occasionally it is convenient to use several different data
structures as a template for the same underlying machine
representation. A type converter can be used for this
purpose, as in the following example:

```
TYPE
          STRING RECORD [LEN BYTE
                             CHARS ARRAY [255 BYTE]]
          PERSON RECORD [NAME ARRAY [10 BYTE]
                             AGE WORD]
          STRPTR ↑STRING
          PERPTR ↑PERSON
INTERNAL
          S STRPTR
          P PERPTR
          BUFFER ARRAY [1000 BYTE]
             .
             .
             .
          S := STRPTR #BUFFER[0]
          IF S↑.LEN > 128 THEN ...
             .
             .
             .
          P := PERPTR #BUFFER[0]
          IF P↑.NAME[0] = 'A' THEN ...
```

8.2 PROCEDURE INVOCATION

A procedure invocation specifies the evaluation of a
procedure. It consists of the identifier designating
the procedure and may include a list of actual parameters.
The actual parameters are assigned ("bound") to the
corresponding formal parameters declared in the procedure
declaration (see 10). The correspondence is established
by the positions of the parameters in the lists of the
actual and formal parameters, respectively. Parameters
are passed to the procedure by value only; i.e., the
formal parameter is treated as a local declaration of a
variable whose value is assigned from the actual parameter
list upon entry to the procedure.

Each actual parameter must be an arithmetic expression,
possibly containing other procedure invocations. The
corresponding formal parameter represents a local
variable of the called procedure, and the value of the
expression becomes the initial value of this variable.

The type of the actual parameter must be the same type as
the formal parameter. Since the value of a parameter may
be a pointer to a variable, call by reference can be
accomplished by declaring the formal parameter to be of
type pointer to a particular type, and then passing the
address of a variable of the same type.

The procedure when used in an expression must return
exactly one value of the correct type.

    procedure_invocation   => procedure_identifier
                                    [actual_parm_list]

    actual_parm_list   => '(' parameter* ')'

    parameter   => arithmetic_expression

Example:

Given the following procedure and variable declarations,

```
INTERNAL
    P PROCEDURE (IN1 BYTE,IN2 ↑BYTE)
      RETURNS (VAL BYTE)
      :
      END P

    MASK Y Z BYTE
    ZPTR ↑BYTE
```

some valid expressions are:

```
Y + P(Z,ZPTR)
P(Y,#Z) AND MASK
128 + P(2*P(Y+3,ZPTR),#Z)
```

9. STATEMENTS

Statements denote algorithmic actions, and are said to be
executable.

```
statement => simple_statement
          => structured_statement
```

9.1 SIMPLE STATEMENTS

A simple statement is a statement of which no part
constitutes another statement.

```
simple_statement => assignment_statement
                 => procedure_statement
                 => return_statement
                 => loop_control_statement
```

9.1.1 ASSIGNMENT STATEMENT

The assignment statement serves to replace the current
value of a variable by a new value specified as an
expression.

```
assignment_statement => variable assign_op
                               arithmetic_expression

assign_op            => ':=' | '+=' | '-='
```

The variable and the expression must be of the same type.
The form

```
VAR += EXP
```

is similar to

```
VAR := VAR + EXP
```

while the form

```
VAR -= EXP
```

is similar to

```
VAR := VAR - EXP
```

Notice that VAR is evaluated only once in the '+=' and
'-=' constructs.

Examples:

```
PTR := INC PTR
RECT.AREA := RECT.LENGTH * RECT.WIDTH
GO_AHEAD := STILL_RUNNING AND NO_ERRORS
COUNTDOWN -= 1
CUSTOMER↑.BALANCE += DEPOSIT + INTEREST * DEPOSIT
```

9.1.2 PROCEDURE STATEMENT

The procedure statement causes the execution of the procedure
denoted by a procedure identifier and the assignment of any
returned values. If the declaration of the procedure includes
a RETURNS list, the procedure statement is written as a
special form of the assignment statement. In this case, the
number and type of variables in the list must be the same as
the number and type of variables on the left-hand side of the
procedure statement.

```
procedure_statement
            => [variable variable+ ':=']
                 procedure_invocation

procedure_invocation
            => procedure_identifier [actual_parm_list]
```

Examples:

```
BIG := MAX(X,Y)
INITIALIZE
DAY,MO,YEAR := GET_DATE
PRINT_CHAR(DIGIT+'0')
```

9.1.3 RETURN STATEMENT

The return statement causes execution to leave a procedure
body and return to the statement following the procedure
call in the calling procedure. No return statement is
necessary immediately before the END of a procedure since
one is implicit.

        return_statement => RETURN

9.1.4 LOOP CONTROL STATEMENTS

There are two kinds of loop control statements: the exit
and repeat statements. The exit statement causes execution
to continue at the first statement following the innermost
DO...OD block which contains the exit statement, whereas
the repeat statement causes execution to continue at the
first statement of the innermost DO...OD block which
contains the repeat statement. Furthermore, the exit and
repeat statements may be qualified by a label identifier
indicating a specific enclosing DO..OD block to which
execution is to proceed (see 9.2.2).

    loop_control_statement
                        => exit_statement
                        => repeat_statement

    exit_statement   => EXIT [FROM label]

    repeat_statement   => REPEAT [FROM label]

Examples:

        EXIT
        REPEAT FROM ILOOP

9.2 STRUCTURED STATEMENTS

Structured statements are constructs composed of other
statements that are executed either conditionally
(conditional statements) or repeatedly (loop statements).
The syntax of PLZ enables the elimination of the compound
statement, since statements that are to be executed
sequentially in the context of a structured statement are
bracketed by the delimiters of that structured statement.

        structured_statement => conditional_statement
                             => loop_statement

9.2.1 CONDITIONAL STATEMENTS

A conditional statement selects for execution one or more
of its component statements.

        conditional_statement => if_statement
                                => select_statement

9.2.1.1 IF STATEMENT

The if statement specifies that the statements between the
symbols THEN and ELSE (or FI, if there is no ELSE clause)
are to be executed only if a certain conditional expression
is true. If it is false, then either no statement is to
be executed, or, if present, the statements between the
symbols ELSE and FI are to be executed.

        if_statement => IF conditional_expression THEN
                           statement*
                        [ELSE
                           statement*]
                        FI

Note that the only time an expression which contains a
relational operator (see 8.1.1) may appear is in the
if statement. The relational operators do not generate
a data value; nevertheless, the compiler can generate
code to determine whether the comparison is true or
false and thus execute the correct set of statements
in the if statement.

The ANDIF and ORIF operators may be used to compose several
relational expressions, allowing partial evaluation of the
conditional expression. If the left operand of ANDIF is
false, then the right operand is not evaluated. If the
left operand of ORIF is true, then the right operand is

not evaluated. The precedence of the ANDIF, ORIF and
relational operators is described in section 8.1. For
example:

```
IF PTR = NIL ORIF PTR↑.VAL = KEY THEN EXIT
ELSE PTR := PTR↑.NEXT
FI

IF ELEMSIZE > 0 ANDIF TBLSIZE/ELEMSIZE > 2 THEN
    SUBDIVIDE(TABLE)
FI
```

Notice that in the first example, PTR should not be used
to reference a record field when its value is NIL, while
a division by zero is avoided in the second example.

Examples:

```
IF A[I] > A[J] THEN
    TEMP := A[I]
    A[I] := A[J]
    A[J] := TEMP
FI

IF I <= 5 THEN
    PROCESS(1)
ELSE
    IF I <= 8 THEN
        PROCESS(2)
    ELSE
        IF I < 13 THEN
            PROCESS(3)
        ELSE
            PROCESS(4)
        FI
    FI
FI


IF PRIORITY = 0 ORIF
    WAIT_ON_IO=TRUE ANDIF EMPTY(READYQ)=FALSE THEN
        RUN(TCB[I])
ELSE
    DO !BUSY WAIT!
    OD
FI
```

9.2.1.2 SELECT STATEMENT

The select statement is an extension of the if statement
and consists of an expression (the selector) and a list of
select elements of the form

      CASE constant_expression+ THEN statement*

where the constant expressions may be given in any order.
It specifies that the statements of the one select element,
whose list of constant expressions contains the current
value of the selector, are to be executed. Thus, constant
expressions evaluating to the same constant may not appear
in different select elements. An ELSE clause can be used
to identify those statements which should be executed if
none of the constant expressions equals the current value
of the selector. If none of the constant expressions
equals the selector and there is no ELSE clause, no
statements in the body of the select statement are
executed. Each element is terminated by the next select
element. The ELSE clause, if present, is terminated by
the select statement terminator FI.

```
        select_statement => IF arithmetic_expression
                               select_element+
                               [ELSE statement*]
                               FI

        select_element   => CASE select_expression+ THEN
                               statement*

        select_expression
                         => constant_expression
```

Examples:

```
IF SYMTYPE[NEXT SYMBOL]
CASE 1 THEN SCANDIGIT
            VAL := STR_TO_INT(STARTPTR, ENDPTR)
CASE 2 THEN SCANID
CASE 3 THEN SCANOP
CASE TAB, BLANK THEN SCANDELIM
CASE ',' ';' ':' THEN SCANPUNCTUATION
ELSE ILLEGAL
FI



IF COMMANDLETTER
CASE ESC THEN QUIT RETURN
CASE 'P', 'p' THEN PASTE (CURSOR1, CURSOR2)
CASE 'C', 'c' THEN CUT (CURSOR1, CURSOR2)
CASE 'I', 'i' THEN
            UPDATE (CURSOR1)
            IF CURWINDOW
            CASE COMMANDW   THEN EXPANDNAME('I')
                                 INPUT(KEYBOARD)
            CASE USERW      THEN INPUT(KEYBOARD)
                                 IF EOF=TRUE THEN
                                      ERROR(EMPTY)
                                 FI
            CASE RECOVERYW  THEN UPDATE(CURSOR2)
                                 UNDO

            FI
ELSE ERROR(UNRECOGNIZED)
FI
```

9.2.2 LOOP STATEMENT

The only framework provided for repetitive statements in
PLZ is the loop statement. The statements between the
symbols DO and OD are executed repeatedly until control is
diverted through a loop control statement. The exit,
repeat, or return statements are the only way to change
the flow of execution through the statements delimited by
the symbols DO and OD. The exit and repeat statements may,
of course, appear in conditional statements, thus providing
the capability to effect the well-known FOR, WHILE, and
UNTIL constructs.

A DO statement does not introduce a new scope; no new
identifiers can be declared.

```
loop_statement => [label] DO statement* OD

label           => identifier
```

Examples:

```
!Nested "FOR" loops, with a 2-level exit!
   I := 1
   ILOOP: DO
      IF I > LIMI THEN EXIT FI
      J := 1
      JLOOP: DO
         IF J > LIMJ THEN EXIT FI
         IF A[I,J] = TERMINATOR THEN EXIT FROM ILOOP FI
         J := J+1
      OD
      I := I+1
   OD
   !When we get here, either a[i,j] = terminator, or
   i > limi and j > limj!

!WHILE COND DO...loop!
DO
   IF COND = FALSE THEN EXIT FI
   .
   .
   .
OD
```

```
!REPEAT...UNTIL COND loop!
DO
   .
   .
   IF COND = TRUE THEN EXIT FI
OD

!non-repetitive sequence!
DO
    .
    .
    .
   EXIT
OD

!infinite loop!
DO
OD


!Use REPEAT FROM to find a matching row!
   I := 0
   MATCH_ROW := 0
   ILOOP: DO
      I += 1
      IF I > LIMI THEN EXIT FI
      J := 0
      JLOOP: DO
         J += 1
         IF J > COMPLIST_SIZE THEN
            EXIT
         FI
         IF A[I,J] <> COMPLIST[J] THEN
            REPEAT FROM ILOOP
         FI
      OD
      !We get here only if j > complist_size,
       i.e., a[i,j] = complist [j], for all j
       such that 1 <= j <= complist_size!
      MATCH_ROW := I
      EXIT
   OD
      !Either i > limi and no rows matched
       (match_row = 0), or 1 <= i <= limi and
       match_row = i!
```

10. PROCEDURE DECLARATIONS

A procedure declaration serves to define an executable part
of a program, and to associate an identifier with it so
that it can be activated by procedure statements or
procedure invocations in expressions.

The procedure heading specifies the identifier naming the
procedure, the formal parameter identifiers (if any), and
the identifiers whose values are to be returned (if any).
The formal parameters are also referred to as "in"
parameters since their values are considered input values
to the procedure, while the term "out" parameters refers to
the returned values which are considered output values of
the procedure. All such identifiers are considered local
to the procedure body. The base type of a parameter may
be any simple type. Thus arrays and records may not be
passed, but pointers to these structures are allowed
as parameters.

Procedures may return values of any assignable type (see
9.1.2). The value or values returned are the current values
of the identifiers specified in the RETURNS list of the
procedure heading at the time that a RETURN or END
statement is executed. The RETURN statement itself does not
specify the value to be returned.

A procedure declaration may also include LOCAL variable
declarations which associate identifiers with storage that
is dynamically allocated on each procedure entry. Thus
recursion and re-entrant procedures are possible, and the
storage usage of a program may vary during execution so
that a program can be designed to use less data storage
than one whose allocation is completely static. Local
variables may be of any type and their scope is local to
the containing procedure. Local variables may not be
initialized since they are allocated each time the
procedure is entered.

A procedure is activated by the evaluation of a procedure
invocation. If the procedure returns a single value, then
its invocation may be used either in an expression or in a
procedure statement. If it returns either no values or more
than one value, the procedure invocation may appear only in
a procedure statement (see sections 8.2 and 9.1.2).

Occurrence of a procedure identifier in an expression or a
procedure statement within its declaration implies the
recursive execution of the procedure.

All procedures must be declared before they are used. If
two procedures are mutually recursive (that is, a
procedure calls another procedure, which in turn results

in the invocation of the first procedure), then it is
not possible to give both declarations before their
usage in the same module. This problem may be
overcome by placing the declarations in separate
modules, using the appropriate GLOBAL and EXTERNAL
declaration classes for the procedures.

```
        procedure_declaration
                    => procedure_identifier
                            PROCEDURE [formal_parm_list]
                                [RETURNS formal_parm_list]
                            locals*
                            [ENTRY
                                statement*]
                            END procedure_identifier

        formal_parm_list => '(' formal_parm* ')'

        formal_parm      => identifier+ simple_type

        locals           => LOCAL
                                (identifier+ type)*
```

Notice that the keyword ENTRY is used to separate the
declarations of parameters and local variables from the
executable sequence of statements that constitutes the body
of the procedure.

Example:

```
TYPE
    TABLE ARRAY [30 BYTE]
    TABLEPTR ↑TABLE
INTERNAL
    CH RESULT BYTE
    T  TABLE
    TPTR TABLEPTR := #T   !Initialize pointer to table!

    VERIFY PROCEDURE (CHAR BYTE, PTR TABLEPTR)
          RETURNS (RSLT BYTE)
        ! Check whether CHAR is in TABLE
          pointed to by PTR !

        LOCAL
            INDEX BYTE
        ENTRY
          INDEX := 0
          DO
            IF INDEX = 30 THEN RSLT := FALSE EXIT FI
            IF CHAR = PTR↑[INDEX] THEN
                        RSLT := TRUE EXIT
            FI
            INDEX += 1
          OD
        END VERIFY
```

A call to VERIFY looks like:

```
RESULT := VERIFY (CH, TPTR)
```

The declaration of an EXTERNAL procedure contains only
the procedure heading, since the actual executable body
is defined in another module where the procedure is
declared GLOBAL. Since references to the formal parameter
names do not occur in an EXTERNAL procedure declaration, the
names may optionally be omitted, however the types are
required. For example, in the recommended form:

```
EXTERNAL
GETSEQ PROCEDURE (UNIT BYTE
                  BUFPTR ↑BYTE
                  NUMBYTES WORD)
        RETURNS  (RETBYTES WORD
                  RCODE BYTE)
```

could also be written:

```
EXTERNAL
GETSEQ PROCEDURE (BYTE ↑BYTE WORD)
        RETURNS  (WORD BYTE)
```

```
restricted_procedure_declaration
                => procedure_identifier
                    PROCEDURE [parameter_type_list]
                    [RETURNS parameter_type_list]

parameter_type_list => '(' restricted_parm* ')'

restricted_parm      => identifier* simple_type
```

The following example demonstrates the use of recursion
and the ordering of procedure declarations before their
usage.

```
EXTERNAL
    PUTCH PROCEDURE (CH BYTE)
    PUTSTRING PROCEDURE (START ↑BYTE, COUNT BYTE)

INTERNAL

! print non-negative decimal integer
  with leading zeros suppressed !

    NPRINT PROCEDURE (N INTEGER)
        ENTRY
            IF N>0 THEN
                NPRINT(N/10)
                PUTCH(BYTE(N MOD 10)+'0')
            FI
        END NPRINT

GLOBAL
    PRINTDEC PROCEDURE (N INTEGER)
        ENTRY
            IF N>0 THEN NPRINT(N)
            ELSE
                IF N=0 THEN PUTCH('0')
                ELSE PUTCH('-')
                    IF N=-32768 THEN
                        PUTSTRING(#'32768',5)
                    ELSE
                        NPRINT(ABS N)
                    FI
                FI
            FI
        END PRINTDEC
```

11. PROGRAMS AND MODULES

A PLZ program consists of a sequence of modules to be
linked together by the available linking facility. The
name of a GLOBAL procedure should be supplied to the
linking facility to specify the entry point of a PLZ
program. The parameters to this procedure are defined by
the particular system where the program is executed.

A PLZ module consists of a sequence of variable and
procedure declarations (i.e., executable statements appear
only inside procedure declarations). In addition to
parameter passing between procedures, the sharing of data
(or procedures) between modules may be achieved by
declaring a variable (procedure) to be GLOBAL in one module
and declaring references to that variable (procedure)
within other modules as EXTERNAL. Data (procedures) which
are declared INTERNAL to a module may be referenced only
within that module.

A SAMPLE PROGRAM

The following program accepts text from the console (each
"token" is a string of characters separated by a blank) and
produces an alphabetized list of all the tokens input up to
a return character. The algorithm uses a binary tree
of tokens where the left subtree of each token is
alphabetically less than the given token, and the right
subtree has all the tokens whch are greater than or equal.
The printing routine recursively traverses the tree to
output the alphabetized list.

The program consists of three modules: the main treesort
module, a storage allocator module and an I/O module which
is not shown. The two I/O procedures getseq (which reads a
sequence of bytes) and putseq (which writes a sequence of
bytes) are declared as EXTERNAL to the corresponding
modules.

```
treesort module

constant
      TRUE := 1
      FALSE := 0
      CONOUT := 2                ! console output unit !

type
      node record [name ↑byte
                   left, right ↑node]

external
      alloc_node  procedure
                  returns (newnode ↑node) ·
      input_token procedure
                  returns (notdone byte)
      putseq procedure (unit byte, bufptr ↑byte, numbytes word)
             returns (retbytes word, rcode byte)

internal

      putchar procedure (unit, ch byte)
         local length word
               retcode byte
         entry
               length, retcode :=
                     putseq (unit, #ch, 1)
         end putchar

global
      root ↑node := NIL        ! initialize root of tree !

! output string delimited by blank !

      print procedure (bufptr ↑byte)
         entry
               do
                     if bufptr↑ = ' ' then
                                 putchar (CONOUT, '%r')
                                 exit
                     else    putchar (CONOUT, bufptr↑)
                             bufptr := inc bufptr
                     fi
               od
         end print
```

```
internal

! recursive symmetric order traversal routine !

     treeprint procedure (currentnode ↑node)
        entry
                if currentnode↑.left <> NIL then
                        treeprint (currentnode↑.left) fi
                print (currentnode↑.name)
                if currentnode↑.right <> NIL then
                        treeprint (currentnode↑.right) fi
        end treeprint



! string comparison -- returns TRUE if str1 <= str2 !

lessequal procedure (str1, str2 ↑byte)
        returns (order byte)
   entry
        do
        if str1↑ <> str2↑ then
                if str1↑ <= str2↑ then
                        order := TRUE return
                else
                        order := FALSE return
                fi
        else
                if str1↑ = ' ' then
                        order := TRUE return
                else
                        str1 := inc str1
                        str2 := inc str2
                fi
        fi
        od
   end lessequal
```

```
! The workhorse procedure:  traverse tree to find
  appropriate place to insert node.  Names which are
  alphabetically less  are found in the left subtree !

insert procedure
    local newnode, currentnode ↑node
    entry
          newnode := alloc_node
          if newnode <> NIL then
              if root <> NIL then          ! is tree empty? !
                  currentnode := root
                  do
                      if lessequal(newnode↑.name,currentnode↑.name)
                                                     = TRUE then
                          if currentnode↑.left <> NIL then
                                  currentnode := currentnode↑.left
                          else
                                  currentnode↑.left := newnode exit
                          fi
                      else
                          if currentnode↑.right <> NIL then
                                  currentnode := currentnode↑.right
                          else
                                  currentnode↑.right := newnode exit
                          fi
                      fi
                  od
              else
                      root := newnode ! first node in tree !
              fi
          fi
    end insert




! The main procedure inputs tokens and inserts nodes in the
  tree.  When a CR is entered, the alphabetized tree is
  printed !

global
      main procedure
          entry
              do
                  if input_token = TRUE then insert
                  else exit
                  fi
              od
              if root <> NIL then treeprint(root) fi
          end main

end treesort
```

storage module

! contains the storage allocator for nodes and the
  input_token procedure !

```
constant
        TRUE := 1
        FALSE := 0
        MAXNODES := 100
        MAXCHARS := 1500
        CONIN := 1                  ! console input unit !
        CR := '%r'                  ! CR character !
type
        node record [name ↑byte
                       left, right ↑node]
external
        print procedure (bufptr ↑byte)
        getseq procedure (unit byte, bufptr ↑byte, numbytes word)
                returns (retbytes word, rcode byte)
internal
        tree array [MAXNODES node]
        nextnode ↑node := #tree[0]
                ! initialize pointer to first node to be
                   allocated and initialize count of
                   available nodes !
        avail short_integer := MAXNODES

        token ↑byte        ! pointer to start of current token !
                           ! buffer for name strings and index into it !
        stringspace array [MAXCHARS byte]
        nextchar word := 0
        nospacemsg array [* byte] := 'NO_MORE_SPACE '

global

        ! Allocates a node, installs token and initializes
          branches, returning pointer to node.  Outputs
          error message if none are available -- no
          deallocation !

        alloc_node procedure
                returns (newnode ↑node)
           entry
                if avail <> 0 then
                    newnode := nextnode
                    newnode↑.name := token
                    newnode↑.left := NIL
                    newnode↑.right := NIL
                    avail -= 1
                    nextnode := inc nextnode
                else
                    newnode := NIL
                    print (#nospacemsg[0])
                fi
           end alloc_node
```

! reads characters from the console until either a blank
  or a CR, returning notdone = FALSE if a CR, and token
  pointing to start of string delimited by blank !

```
    input_token procedure
            returns (notdone byte)
        local length word
                retcode byte
        entry
                token := #stringspace[nextchar]
                do    ! get 1 character at a time !
                  length, retcode :=
                      getseq (CONIN, #stringspace[nextchar], 1)
                  if stringspace[nextchar] = ' ' then
                    nextchar += 1
                    notdone := TRUE
                    exit
                  else
                    if stringspace[nextchar] = CR then
                          stringspace[nextchar] := ' '
                          notdone := FALSE exit ! replace CR !
                    fi
                  fi
                  if nextchar >= MAXCHARS then
                    print (#nospacemsg[0])
                    notdone := FALSE
                    exit
                  else
                    nextchar += 1
                  fi
                od
        end input_token

end storage
```

12. IMPLEMENTATION NOTES

This section discusses general implementation conventions
and restrictions for parts of the PLZ/SYS language which
should be emphasized.

12.1 IDENTIFIERS AND KEYWORDS

Identifiers may vary in capitalization. The PLZ rule is
that each time an identifier is used, it must be written
the same way it was declared (see 4).

Keywords such as GLOBAL or RETURN may be written in either
entirely capital letters or entirely lower case, thus
either GLOBAL or global is acceptable, but GloBaL would be
taken to be an identifier, not a keyword.

12.2 REPRESENTATION OF POINTERS

The representation of a pointer in memory is independent of
the type of variable to which it points. By their very
nature, address quantities are machine-dependent values.
Thus PLZ/SYS programs which are intended to be
transportable to various machines should limit their use of
pointers to assignment, parameter-passing, and equality
tests and avoid arithmetic operations or assigning constant
values to pointer variables through type conversions.

The representation of the pointer value NIL is implementation
dependent, so portable programs should avoid the use of
comparisons other than equality and inequality. The INC
and DEC operators are not valid when applied to NIL since
the size of the variable pointed to is not defined.

12.3 STRUCTURE ALIGNMENT

Some machines require that data variables be aligned on
certain address boundaries, and therefore record fields may
not necessarily be assigned contiguous memory locations.
The SIZEOF operator may be used to determine the total
number of bytes occupied by a record, which will always
be rounded up to a value which falls on the alignment boundary.
The alignment boundary of a record is taken to be the
maximum alignment boundary of its fields, which depends on
the particular machine. Thus programs which are to be
portable to other translators or machines should not assume
any particular allocation of record fields.

PLZ/SYS does guarantee that elements of a one-dimensional
array are allocated sequential memory locations starting
from the base address of the array. This allows elements
to be accessed by using pointers which are usually more
efficient than array indices on most machines. The user is
cautioned that compiler implementations are not required to
generate code to check that array indices are in bounds for
the declared size of an array, nor is it required that code
be generated to check that the INC or DEC operators applied
to a pointer to an element in an array yields an address
still within the bounds of the array.

12.4 UNARY OPERATORS IN LISTS

PLZ has the characteristic that a list of numbers such as
"4,-2,1" has the perhaps unexpected interpretation of being
only two distinct values (2 and 1), since the comma is
equivalent to a blank throughout PLZ and thus the first two
numbers evaluate to the single expression 4-2. This
interpretation is due to a combination of the lack of any
delineation between elements in a list other than
delimiters, and the ambiguity of using the same symbol "-"
for both unary and binary minus (the same is true for
"+"). While this will usually cause only minor
problems in either parameter lists or array indices
since the compiler checks for the correct number of
values, unexpected results may occur in either a
list of initialization values or in a list of select
expressions following the keyword CASE. There are at least
two simple solutions to avoid this problem: use 0-N
instead of -N whenever it appears in a list of values,
or enclose the expression in parentheses as in "4,(-2),1".

12.5 ONE-PASS COMPILATION

PLZ has been designed to permit one-pass translation. To this
end, identifiers must be declared before they are used.
However, this restriction is relaxed for identifiers following
'↑' in declarations of pointer variables or definitions of
pointer types. The following excerpt from 7.3 illustrates
this:

```
    TYPE
        ENTRY_PTR ↑TABLE_ENTRY
        TABLE_ENTRY RECORD [NAME STRING
                            NEXT ENTRY_PTR]
```

PLZ/SYS GRAMMAR

```
module                  => module_identifier MODULE
                           declarations*
                           END module_identifier

declarations            => constants
                        => types
                        => globals
                        => internals
                        => externals

constants               => CONSTANT
                              constant_definition*

types                   => TYPE
                              type_definition*

globals                 => GLOBAL
                              var_or_proc_declaration*

internals               => INTERNAL
                              var_or_proc_declaration*

externals               => EXTERNAL
                              restricted_var_or_proc_declaration*

constant_definition     => identifier
                              ':=' constant_expression

constant_expression     => constant_term
                              (add_op constant_term)*

constant_term           => constant_factor
                              (mult_op constant_factor)*

constant_factor         => unary_op constant_factor
                        => constant
                        => '(' constant_expression ')'

constant                => number
                        => character_constant
                        => constant_identifier
                        => SIZEOF static_variable
                        => SIZEOF type_identifier
                        => SIZEOF constant_identifier

character_constant      => ''' character_text [character_text] '''

type_definition         => identifier type
```

```
type                        => simple_type
                            => structured_type

simple_type                 => BYTE
                            => WORD
                            => INTEGER
                            => SHORT_INTEGER
                            => pointer_type
                            => simple_type_identifier

pointer_type                => '↑' type
                            => pointer_type_identifier

structured_type             => array_type
                            => record_type

array_type                  => ARRAY '[' constant_expression+ type ']'
                            => array_type_identifier

record_type                 => RECORD '[' field_declaration+ ']'
                            => record_type_identifier

field_declaration           => identifier+ type

var_or_proc_declaration     => variable_declaration
                            => procedure_declaration

restricted_var_or_proc_declaration
                            => identifier+ type
                            => restricted_procedure_declaration

variable_declaration        => identifier simple_type
                                 [ ':=' initial_value ]
                            => identifier identifier+ simple_type
                                 [ ':=' '[' initial_value*
                                              ['...'] ']' ]
                            => identifier structured_type
                                 [ ':=' constructor ]
                            => identifier identifier+ structured_type
                                 [ ':=' '[' constructor*
                                              ['...'] ']' ]
                            => identifier ARRAY '[' '*' simple_type ']'
                                 ':=' '[' initial_value+ ']'
                            => identifier ARRAY '[' '*' simple_type ']'
                                 ':=' text_constant+

constructor                 => '[' initial_component* ['...'] ']'

initial_component           => initial_value
                            => constructor

initial_value               => type_converter initial_value
                            => (INC|DEC) initial_value
                            => constant_expression
                            => '#' static_variable
                            => '#' text_constant
                            => NIL
                            => '?'
```

```
text_constant              => character_sequence

static_variable            => simple_identifier
                           => array_identifier
                           => record_identifier
                           => static_array_variable
                           => static_record_variable

static_array_variable      => static_array_designator
                                  '[' constant_expression+ ']'

static_array_designator    => array_identifier
                           => static_record_variable
                           => static_array_variable

static_record_variable     => static_record_designator
                                  '.' field_identifier

static_record_designator
                           => record_identifier
                           => static_array_variable
                           => static_record_variable

procedure_declaration      => procedure_identifier
                                  PROCEDURE [formal_parm_list]
                                     [RETURNS formal_parm_list]
                                  locals*
                                  [ENTRY
                                     statement*]
                                  END procedure_identifier

formal_parm_list           => '(' formal_parm* ')'

formal_parm                => identifier+ simple_type

locals                     => LOCAL
                                  (identifier+ type)*

restricted_procedure_declaration
                           => procedure_identifier
                                  PROCEDURE [parameter_type_list]
                                     [RETURNS parameter_type_list]

parameter_type_list        => '(' restricted_parm* ')'

restricted_parm            => identifier* simple_type
```

```
statement                   => assignment_statement
                            => if_statement
                            => select_statement
                            => loop_statement
                            => exit_statement
                            => repeat_statement
                            => return_statement
                            => procedure_statement

assignment_statement        => variable assign_op
                                  arithmetic_expression

assign_op                   => ':=' | '+=' | '-='

if_statement                => IF conditional_expression THEN
                                  statement*
                               [ELSE statement*]
                               FI

select_statement            => IF arithmetic_expression
                                  select_element+
                               [ELSE statement*]
                               FI

select_element              => CASE constant_expression+ THEN
                                  statement*

loop_statement              => [label] DO
                                  statement*
                               OD

label                       => identifier

exit_statement              => EXIT [FROM label]

repeat_statement            => REPEAT [FROM label]

return_statement            => RETURN

procedure_statement         => [variable variable+ ':=']
                                  procedure_invocation

procedure_invocation        => procedure_identifier
                                  [actual_parm_list]

actual_parm_list            => '(' parameter* ')'

parameter                   => arithmetic_expression
```

```
conditional_expression   => conditional_term
                               (ORIF conditional_term)*

conditional_term          => conditional_factor
                               (ANDIF conditional_factor)*

conditional_factor        => arithmetic_expression
                               [rel_op arithmetic_expression]

arithmetic_expression     => arithmetic_term
                               (add_op arithmetic_term)*

arithmetic_term           => arithmetic_factor
                               (mult_op arithmetic_factor)*

arithmetic_factor         => unary_operator arithmetic_factor
                          => constant
                          => variable
                          => '#' variable
                          => '#' text_constant
                          => NIL
                          => '(' conditional_expression ')'

rel_op                    => '=' | '<>' | '<' | '>' | '<=' | '>='

add_op                    => '+' | '-' | OR | XOR

mult_op                   => '*' | '/' | MOD | AND

unary_operator            => unary_op
                          => type_converter

unary_op                  => '+' | '-' | ABS | NOT | INC | DEC

type_converter            => BYTE
                          => WORD
                          => SHORT_INTEGER
                          => INTEGER
                          => type_identifier
```

```
variable                    => identifier
                            => procedure_invocation
                            => array_variable
                            => record_variable
                            => pointer_variable

array_variable              => array_designator
                                 '[T arithmetic_expression+ ']'

array_designator            => variable

record_variable             => record_designator '.' field_identifier

record_designator           => variable

pointer_variable            => pointer_designator '↑'

pointer_designator          => variable
```

PLZ/SYS LEXICAL GRAMMAR

```
PLZ_text                  => separator* [id_constant_text]
                                (separator+ id_constant_text)*

id_constant_text          => identifier
                          => word_symbol
                          => literal_constant

separator                 => delimiter_text
                          => special_symbol

identifier                => letter (letter | digit | '_')*

literal_constant          => number
                          => character_sequence

delimiter_text            => delimiter
                          => comment

number                    => integer
                          => hex_number

integer                   => digit+

hex_number                => '%' hex_digit+

character_sequence        => ''' character_text+ '''

character_text            => character
                          => special_character_text

character                 => any_character_except_%_or_'

special_character_text    => '%' special_character
                          => '%' hex_digit hex_digit

special_character         => 'R' | 'L' | 'T' | 'P' | 'Q' | '%'
                          => 'r' | 'l' | 't' | 'p' | 'q'

comment                   => comment_initiator comment_char*
                                comment_terminator

comment_char              => any_character_except_comment_terminator

comment_initiator         => '|'

comment_terminator        => '|'

letter                    => 'A' | 'B' | ... | 'Z'
                          => 'a' | 'b' | ... | 'z'
```

```
digit                    => '0' | '1' | ... | '9'

hex_digit                => digit
                         => 'A' | 'B' | ... | 'F'
                         => 'a' | 'b' | ... | 'f'

special_symbol           => '+' | '-' | '*' | '/' | '='
                         => '<' | '>' | '<=' | '>=' | '<>'
                         => '.' | '%' | '↑' | ':=' | '+='
                         => '-=' | '#" | '[' | ']' | '(' | ')'
                         => '?' | '...'

word_symbol              => ABS | AND | ANDIF | ARRAY | BYTE
                         => CASE | CONSTANT | DEC | DO | ELSE
                         => END | ENTRY | EXIT | EXTERNAL | FI
                         => FROM | GLOBAL | IF | INC | INTEGER
                         => INTERNAL | LOCAL | MOD | MODULE | NIL
                         => NOT | OD | OR | ORIF | PROCEDURE
                         => RECORD | REPEAT | RETURN | RETURNS
                         => SHORT_INTEGER | SIZEOF | THEN
                         => TYPE ⊤ WORD | XOR

delimiter                => ',' | ';' | ':' | space
                         => tab | formfeed | linefeed
                         => carriage_return
```

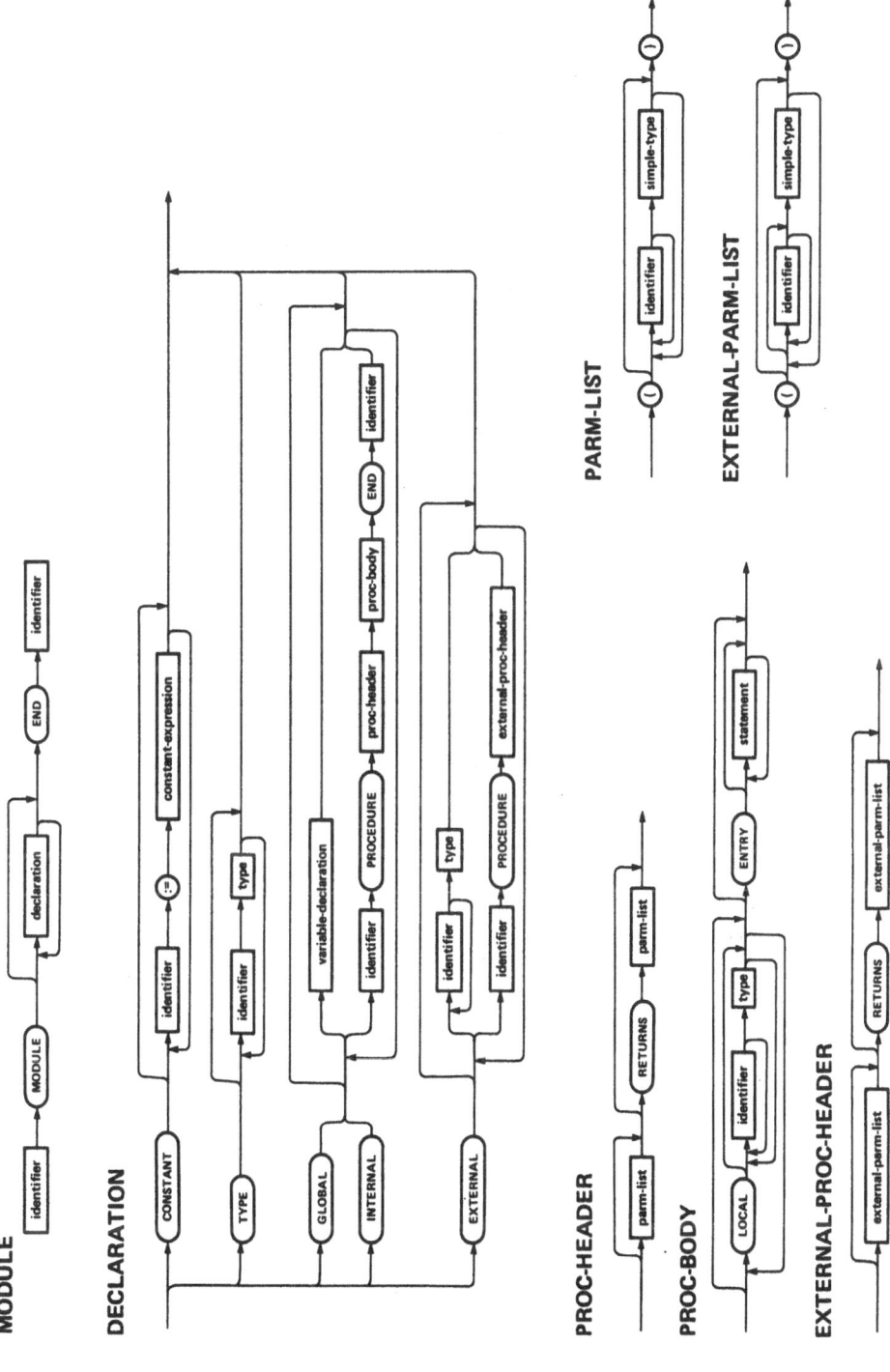

MODULE

DECLARATION

PARM-LIST

EXTERNAL-PARM-LIST

PROC-HEADER

PROC-BODY

EXTERNAL-PROC-HEADER

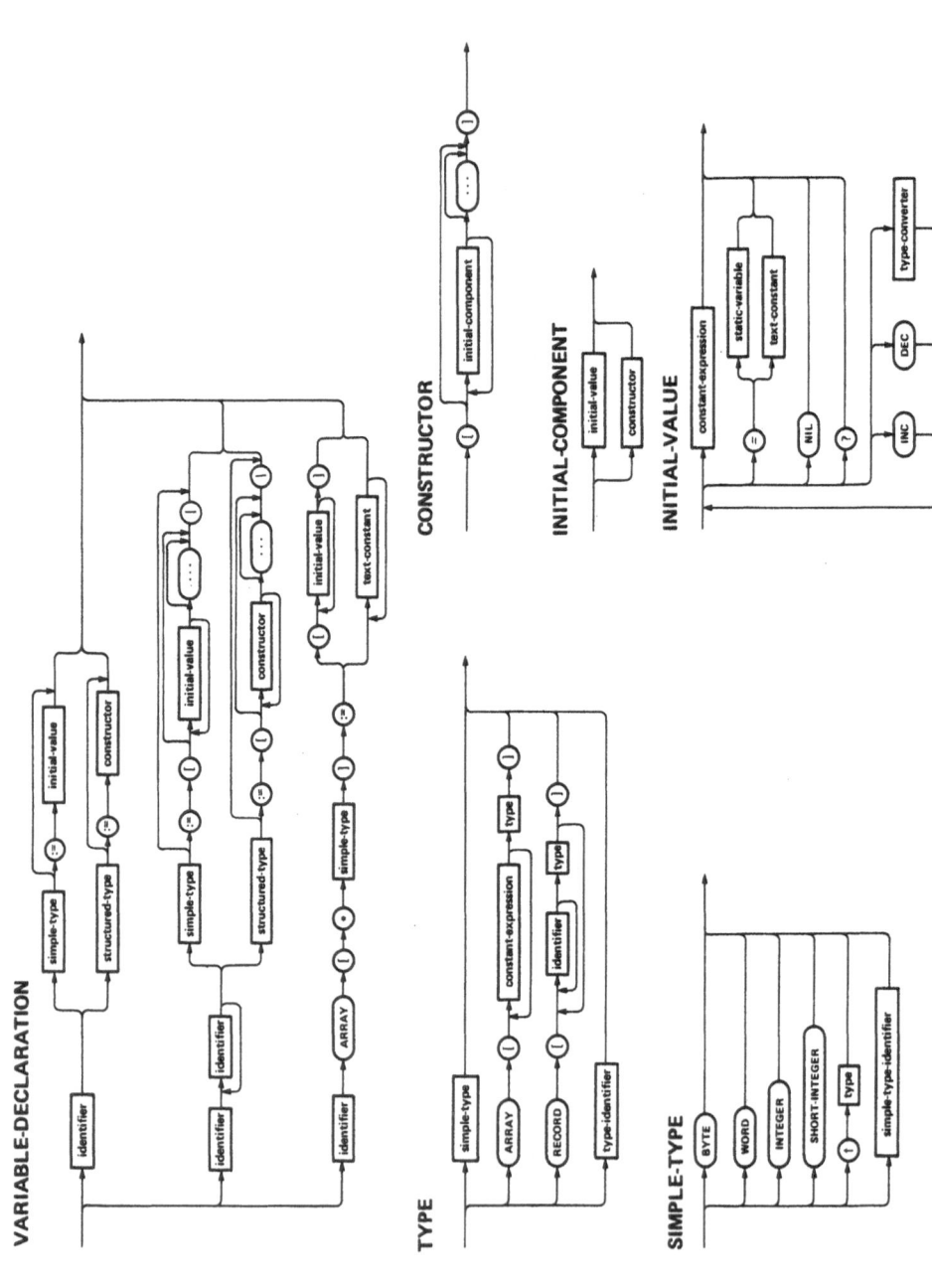

VARIABLE-DECLARATION

CONSTRUCTOR

INITIAL-COMPONENT

INITIAL-VALUE

TYPE

SIMPLE-TYPE

STATEMENT

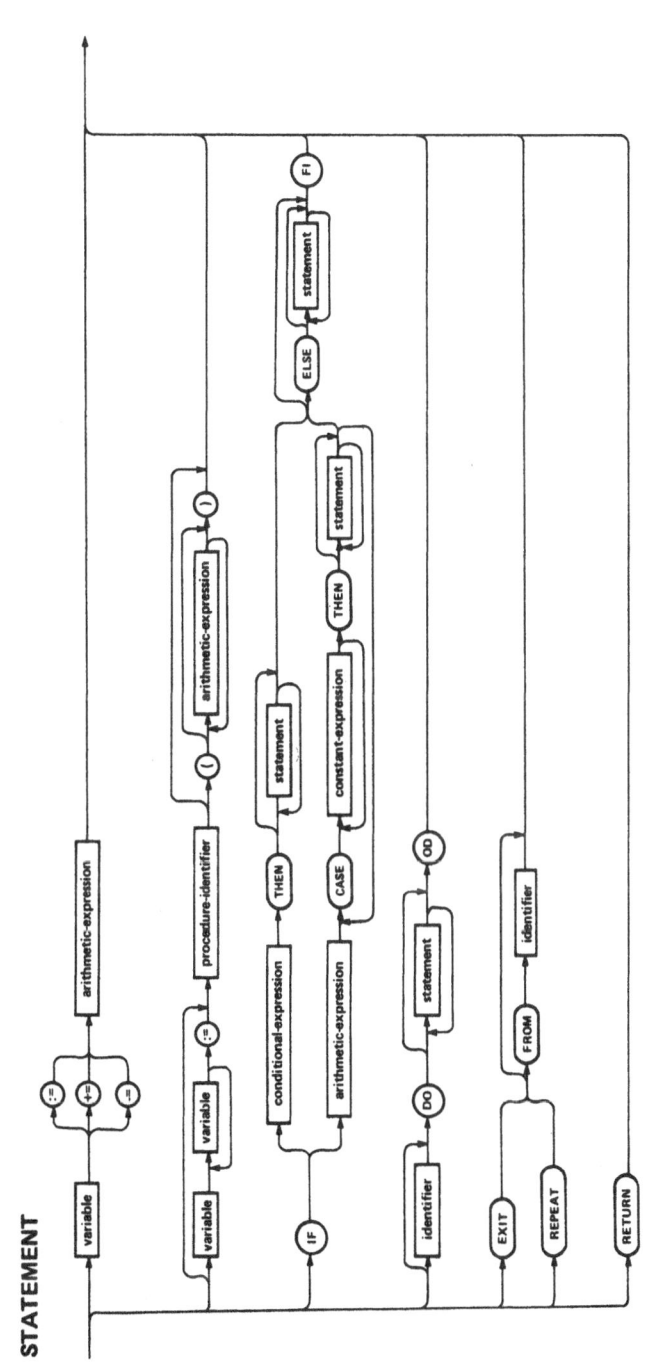

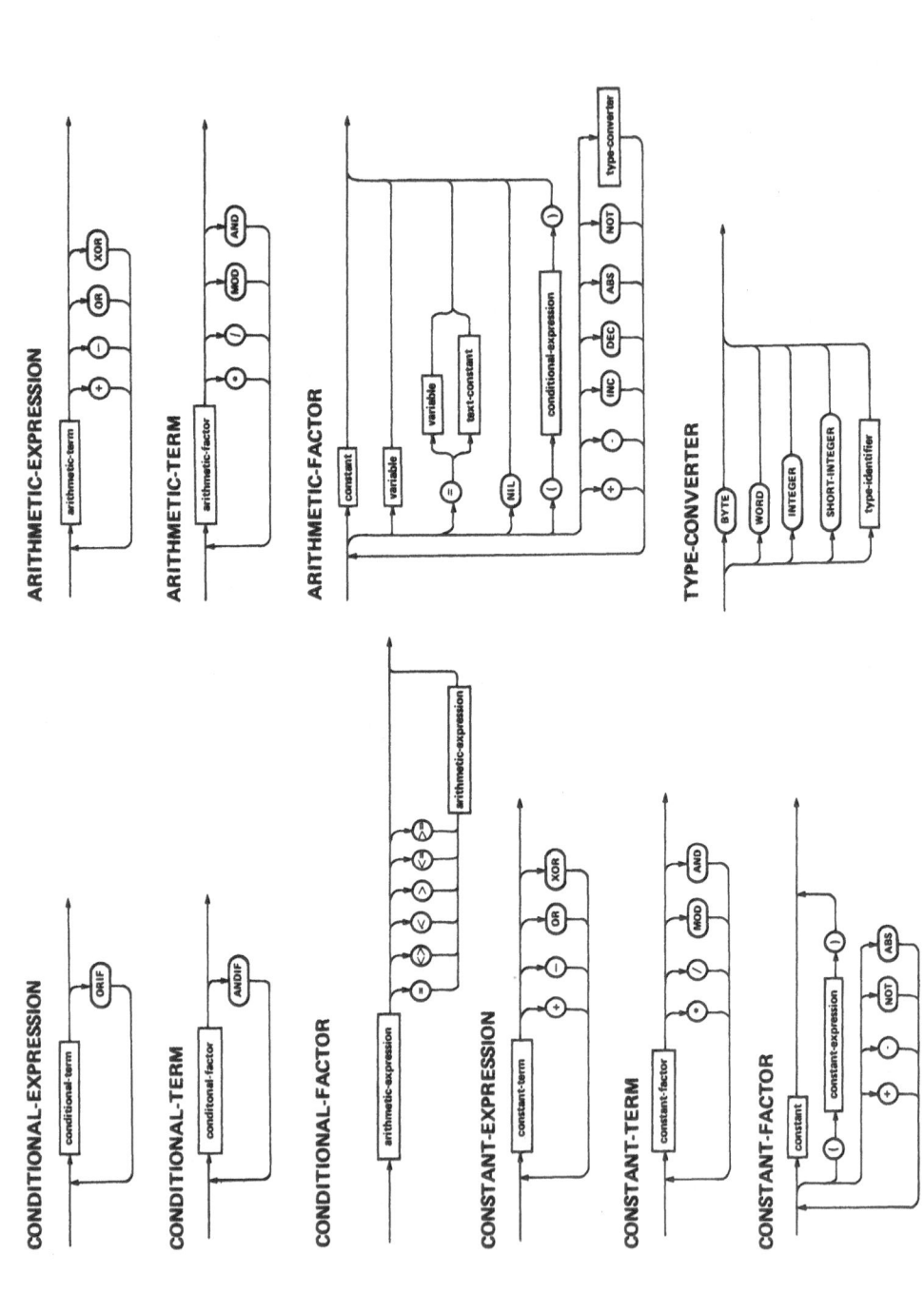

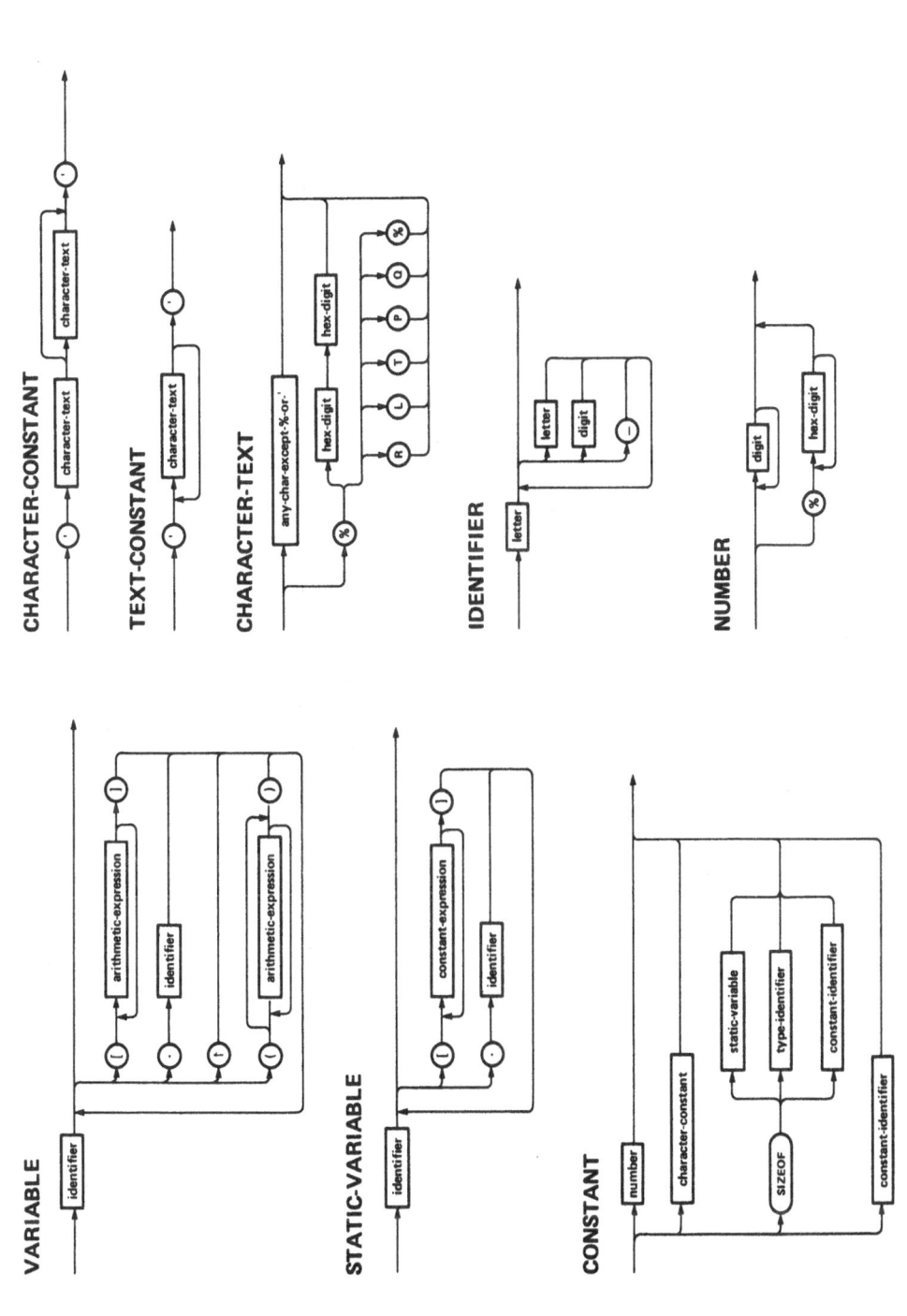